Italo Calvino was born in Cuba in 1923 and grew up in San Remo, Italy. He was an essayist and journalist as well as a novelist and was a member of the editorial staff of the Turin publishing firm Giulio Einaudi editore. In 1973 he won the prestigious Italian literary award the Premio Feltrinelli. His previous books include *The Castle of Crossed Destinies*, *Invisible Cities*, *Our Ancestors*, *Adam, One Afternoon*, *If on a Winter's Night a Traveller*, *Marcovaldo*, *Mr Palomar*, *The Literature Machine* and *Time & The Hunter*.

Italo Calvino died in 1985.

ITALO CALVINO

Cosmi-Comics

TRANSLATED FROM THE ITALIAN BY
WILLIAM WEAVER

in association with Jonathan Cape

First published in Great Britain by Jonathan Cape Ltd 1969

This Picador edition published 1993 by Pan Books Ltd,
Cavaye Place, London SW10 9PG
in association with Jonathan Cape Ltd

3 5 7 9 8 6 4 2

'All at One Point' and 'Games Without End' originally appeared in
Playboy Magazine

Printed and bound in Great Britain by
Cox & Wyman Ltd, Reading, Berkshire

ISBN 0 330 31908 6

CONTENTS

THE DISTANCE OF
THE MOON

At one time, according to Sir *George H. Darwin, the Moon was very close to the Earth. Then the tides gradually pushed her far away: the tides that the Moon herself causes in the Earth's waters, where the Earth slowly loses energy.*

How well I know!—*old Qfwfq cried,*—the rest of you can't remember, but I can. We had her on top of us all the time, that enormous Moon: when she was full—nights as bright as day, but with a butter-colored light—it looked as if she were going to crush us; when she was new, she rolled around the sky like a black umbrella blown by the wind; and when she was waxing, she came forward with her horns so low she seemed about to stick into the peak of a promontory and get caught there. But the whole business of the Moon's phases worked in a different way then: because the distances from the Sun were different, and the orbits, and the angle of something or other, I forget what; as for eclipses, with Earth and Moon stuck together the way they were, why, we had eclipses every minute: naturally, those two big monsters managed to put each other in the shade constantly, first one, then the other.

Orbit? Oh, elliptical, of course: for a while it would huddle against us and then it would take flight for a while. The tides, when the Moon swung closer, rose so high nobody could hold them back. There were nights when the Moon was full and very, very low, and the tide was so high that the Moon missed a ducking in the sea by a hair's-breadth; well, let's say a few yards anyway. Climb up on the Moon? Of course we did. All you had to do was row out to it in a boat and, when you were underneath, prop a ladder against her and scramble up.

The spot where the Moon was lowest, as she went by, was off the Zinc Cliffs. We used to go out with those little rowboats

3

they had in those days, round and flat, made of cork. They held quite a few of us: me, Captain Vhd Vhd, his wife, my deaf cousin, and sometimes little Xlthlx—she was twelve or so at that time. On those nights the water was very calm, so silvery it looked like mercury, and the fish in it, violet-colored, unable to resist the Moon's attraction, rose to the surface, all of them, and so did the octopuses and the saffron medusas. There was always a flight of tiny creatures—little crabs, squid, and even some weeds, light and filmy, and coral plants—that broke from the sea and ended up on the Moon, hanging down from that lime-white ceiling, or else they stayed in midair, a phosphorescent swarm we had to drive off, waving banana leaves at them.

This is how we did the job: in the boat we had a ladder: one of us held it, another climbed to the top, and a third, at the oars, rowed until we were right under the Moon; that's why there had to be so many of us (I only mentioned the main ones). The man at the top of the ladder, as the boat approached the Moon, would become scared and start shouting: "Stop! Stop! I'm going to bang my head!" That was the impression you had, seeing her on top of you, immense, and all rough with sharp spikes and jagged, saw-tooth edges. It may be different now, but then the Moon, or rather the bottom, the underbelly of the Moon, the part that passed closest to the Earth and almost scraped it, was covered with a crust of sharp scales. It had come to resemble the belly of a fish, and the smell too, as I recall, if not downright fishy, was faintly similar, like smoked salmon.

In reality, from the top of the ladder, standing erect on the last rung, you could just touch the Moon if you held your arms up. We had taken the measurements carefully (we didn't yet suspect that she was moving away from us); the only thing you had to be very careful about was where you put your hands. I always chose a scale that seemed fast (we climbed up in groups of five or six at a time), then I would cling first with one hand, then with both, and immediately I would feel ladder and boat drifting away from below me, and the motion of the Moon would tear me from the Earth's attraction. Yes, the Moon was so strong that she pulled you up; you realized this

4

the moment you passed from one to the other: you had to swing up abruptly, with a kind of somersault, grabbing the scales, throwing your legs over your head, until your feet were on the Moon's surface. Seen from the Earth, you looked as if you were hanging there with your head down, but for you, it was the normal position, and the only odd thing was that when you raised your eyes you saw the sea above you, glistening, with the boat and the others upside down, hanging like a bunch of grapes from the vine.

My cousin, the Deaf One, showed a special talent for making those leaps. His clumsy hands, as soon as they touched the lunar surface (he was always the first to jump up from the ladder), suddenly became deft and sensitive. They found immediately the spot where he could hoist himself up; in fact just the pressure of his palms seemed enough to make him stick to the satellite's crust. Once I even thought I saw the Moon come toward him, as he held out his hands.

He was just as dextrous in coming back down to Earth, an operation still more difficult. For us, it consisted in jumping, as high as we could, our arms upraised (seen from the Moon, that is, because seen from the Earth it looked more like a dive, or like swimming downwards, arms at our sides), like jumping up from the Earth in other words, only now we were without the ladder, because there was nothing to prop it against on the Moon. But instead of jumping with his arms out, my cousin bent toward the Moon's surface, his head down as if for a somersault, then made a leap, pushing with his hands. From the boat we watched him, erect in the air as if he were supporting the Moon's enormous ball and were tossing it, striking it with his palms; then, when his legs came within reach, we managed to grab his ankles and pull him down on board.

Now, you will ask me what in the world we went up on the Moon for; I'll explain it to you. We went to collect the milk, with a big spoon and a bucket. Moon-milk was very thick, like a kind of cream cheese. It formed in the crevices between one scale and the next, through the fermentation of various bodies and substances of terrestrial origin which had flown up from

5

the prairies and forests and lakes, as the Moon sailed over them. It was composed chiefly of vegetal juices, tadpoles, bitumen, lentils, honey, starch crystals, sturgeon eggs, molds, pollens, gelatinous matter, worms, resins, pepper, mineral salts, combustion residue. You had only to dip the spoon under the scales that covered the Moon's scabby terrain, and you brought it out filled with that precious muck. Not in the pure state, obviously; there was a lot of refuse. In the fermentation (which took place as the Moon passed over the expanses of hot air above the deserts) not all the bodies melted; some remained stuck in it: fingernails and cartilage, bolts, sea horses, nuts and peduncles, shards of crockery, fishhooks, at times even a comb. So this paste, after it was collected, had to be refined, filtered. But that wasn't the difficulty: the hard part was transporting it down to the Earth. This is how we did it: we hurled each spoonful into the air with both hands, using the spoon as a catapult. The cheese flew, and if we had thrown it hard enough, it stuck to the ceiling, I mean the surface of the sea. Once there, it floated, and it was easy enough to pull it into the boat. In this operation, too, my deaf cousin displayed a special gift; he had strength and a good aim; with a single, sharp throw, he could send the cheese straight into a bucket we held up to him from the boat. As for me, I occasionally misfired; the contents of the spoon would fail to overcome the Moon's attraction and they would fall back into my eye.

I still haven't told you everything about the things my cousin was good at. That job of extracting lunar milk from the Moon's scales was child's play to him: instead of the spoon, at times he had only to thrust his bare hand under the scales, or even one finger. He didn't proceed in any orderly way, but went to isolated places, jumping from one to the other, as if he were playing tricks on the Moon, surprising her, or perhaps tickling her. And wherever he put his hand, the milk spurted out as if from a nanny goat's teats. So the rest of us had only to follow him and collect with our spoons the substance that he was pressing out, first here, then there, but always as if by chance, since the Deaf One's movements seemed to have no clear, practical sense.

6

There were places, for example, that he touched merely for the fun of touching them: gaps between two scales, naked and tender folds of lunar flesh. At times my cousin pressed not only his fingers but—in a carefully gauged leap—his big toe (he climbed onto the Moon barefoot) and this seemed to be the height of amusement for him, if we could judge by the chirping sounds that came from his throat as he went on leaping.

The soil of the Moon was not uniformly scaly, but revealed irregular bare patches of pale, slippery clay. These soft areas inspired the Deaf One to turn somersaults or to fly almost like a bird, as if he wanted to impress his whole body into the Moon's pulp. As he ventured farther in this way, we lost sight of him at one point. On the Moon there were vast areas we had never had any reason or curiosity to explore, and that was where my cousin vanished; I had suspected that all those somersaults and nudges he indulged in before our eyes were only a preparation, a prelude to something secret meant to take place in the hidden zones.

We fell into a special mood on those nights off the Zinc Cliffs: gay, but with a touch of suspense, as if inside our skulls, instead of the brain, we felt a fish, floating, attracted by the Moon. And so we navigated, playing and singing. The Captain's wife played the harp; she had very long arms, silvery as eels on those nights, and armpits as dark and mysterious as sea urchins; and the sound of the harp was sweet and piercing, so sweet and piercing it was almost unbearable, and we were forced to let out long cries, not so much to accompany the music as to protect our hearing from it.

Transparent medusas rose to the sea's surface, throbbed there a moment, then flew off, swaying toward the Moon. Little Xlthlx amused herself by catching them in midair, though it wasn't easy. Once, as she stretched her little arms out to catch one, she jumped up slightly and was also set free. Thin as she was, she was an ounce or two short of the weight necessary for the Earth's gravity to overcome the Moon's attraction and bring her back: so she flew up among the medusas, suspended over the sea. She took fright, cried, then laughed and started playing,

7

catching shellfish and minnows as they flew, sticking some into her mouth and chewing them. We rowed hard, to keep up with the child: the Moon ran off in her ellipse, dragging that swarm of marine fauna through the sky, and a train of long, entwined seaweeds, and Xlthlx hanging there in the midst. Her two wispy braids seemed to be flying on their own, outstretched toward the Moon; but all the while she kept wriggling and kicking at the air, as if she wanted to fight that influence, and her socks— she had lost her shoes in the flight—slipped off her feet and swayed, attracted by the Earth's force. On the ladder, we tried to grab them.

The idea of eating the little animals in the air had been a good one; the more weight Xlthlx gained, the more she sank toward the Earth; in fact, since among those hovering bodies hers was the largest, mollusks and seaweeds and plankton began to gravitate about her, and soon the child was covered with siliceous little shells, chitinous carapaces, and fibers of sea plants. And the farther she vanished into that tangle, the more she was freed of the Moon's influence, until she grazed the surface of the water and sank into the sea.

We rowed quickly, to pull her out and save her: her body had remained magnetized, and we had to work hard to scrape off all the things encrusted on her. Tender corals were wound about her head, and every time we ran the comb through her hair there was a shower of crayfish and sardines; her eyes were sealed shut by limpets clinging to the lids with their suckers; squids' tentacles were coiled around her arms and her neck; and her little dress now seemed woven only of weeds and sponges. We got the worst of it off her, but for weeks afterwards she went on pulling out fins and shells, and her skin, dotted with little diatoms, remained affected forever, looking—to someone who didn't observe her carefully—as if it were faintly dusted with freckles.

This should give you an idea of how the influences of Earth and Moon, practically equal, fought over the space between them. I'll tell you something else: a body that descended to the Earth from the satellite was still charged for a while with lunar force and rejected the attraction of our world. Even I, big and heavy as I was: every time I had been up there, I took a while to get used to the Earth's up and its down, and the others would have to grab my arms and hold me, clinging in a bunch in the swaying boat while I still had my head hanging and my legs stretching up toward the sky.

"Hold on! Hold on to us!" they shouted at me, and in all that groping, sometimes I ended up by seizing one of Mrs. Vhd Vhd's breasts, which were round and firm, and the contact was good and secure and had an attraction as strong as the Moon's or even stronger, especially if I managed, as I plunged down, to put my other arm around her hips, and with this I passed back into our world and fell with a thud into the bottom of the boat, where Captain Vhd Vhd brought me around, throwing a bucket of water in my face.

This is how the story of my love for the Captain's wife began, and my suffering. Because it didn't take me long to realize whom the lady kept looking at insistently: when my cousin's hands clasped the satellite, I watched Mrs. Vhd Vhd, and in her eyes I could read the thoughts that the deaf man's familiarity with the Moon were arousing in her; and when he disappeared in his mysterious lunar explorations, I saw her become restless, as if on pins and needles, and then it was all clear to me, how Mrs. Vhd Vhd was becoming jealous of the Moon and I was jealous of my cousin. Her eyes were made of diamonds, Mrs. Vhd Vhd's; they flared when she looked at the Moon, almost challengingly, as if she were saying: "You shan't have him!" And I felt like an outsider.

The one who least understood all of this was my deaf cousin. When we helped him down, pulling him—as I explained to you—by his legs, Mrs. Vhd Vhd lost all her self-control, doing everything she could to take his weight against her own body, folding her long silvery arms around him; I felt a pang in my heart (the times I clung to her, her body was soft and kind, but not thrust forward, the way it was with my cousin), while he was indifferent, still lost in his lunar bliss.

I looked at the Captain, wondering if he also noticed his

wife's behavior; but there was never a trace of any expression on that face of his, eaten by brine, marked with tarry wrinkles. Since the Deaf One was always the last to break away from the Moon, his return was the signal for the boats to move off. Then, with an unusually polite gesture, Vhd Vhd picked up the harp from the bottom of the boat and handed it to his wife. She was obliged to take it and play a few notes. Nothing could separate her more from the Deaf One than the sound of the harp. I took to singing in a low voice that sad song that goes: "Every shiny fish is floating, floating; and every dark fish is at the bottom, at the bottom of the sea . . ." and all the others, except my cousin, echoed my words.

Every month, once the satellite had moved on, the Deaf One returned to his solitary detachment from the things of the world; only the approach of the full Moon aroused him again. That time I had arranged things so it wasn't my turn to go up, I could stay in the boat with the Captain's wife. But then, as soon as my cousin had climbed the ladder, Mrs. Vhd Vhd said: "This time I want to go up there, too!"

This had never happened before; the Captain's wife had never gone up on the Moon. But Vhd Vhd made no objection, in fact he almost pushed her up the ladder bodily, exclaiming: "Go ahead then!," and we all started helping her, and I held her from behind, felt her round and soft on my arms, and to hold her up I began to press my face and the palms of my hands against her, and when I felt her rising into the Moon's sphere I was heartsick at that lost contact, so I started to rush after her, saying: "I'm going to go up for a while, too, to help out!"

I was held back as if in a vise. "You stay here; you have work to do later," the Captain commanded, without raising his voice.

At that moment each one's intentions were already clear. And yet I couldn't figure things out; even now I'm not sure I've interpreted it all correctly. Certainly the Captain's wife had for a long time been cherishing the desire to go off privately with my cousin up there (or at least to prevent him from going off alone with the Moon), but probably she had a still more ambitious plan, one that would have to be carried out in agreement with the Deaf One: she wanted the two of them to hide up there together and stay on the Moon for a month. But perhaps my cousin, deaf as he was, hadn't understood anything of what she had tried to explain to him, or perhaps he hadn't even realized that he was the object of the lady's desires. And the Captain? He wanted nothing better than to be rid of his wife; in fact, as soon as she was confined up there, we saw him give free rein to his inclinations and plunge into vice, and then we understood why he had done nothing to hold her back. But had he known from the beginning that the Moon's orbit was widening?

None of us could have suspected it. The Deaf One perhaps, but only he: in the shadowy way he knew things, he may have had a presentiment that he would be forced to bid the Moon farewell that night. This is why he hid in his secret places and reappeared only when it was time to come back down on board. It was no use for the Captain's wife to try to follow him: we saw her cross the scaly zone various times, length and breadth, then suddenly she stopped, looking at us in the boat, as if about to ask us whether we had seen him.

Surely there was something strange about that night. The sea's surface, instead of being taut as it was during the full Moon, or even arched a bit toward the sky, now seemed limp, sagging, as if the lunar magnet no longer exercised its full power. And the light, too, wasn't the same as the light of other full Moons; the night's shadows seemed somehow to have thickened. Our friends up there must have realized what was happening; in fact, they looked up at us with frightened eyes. And from their mouths and ours, at the same moment, came a cry: "The Moon's going away!"

The cry hadn't died out when my cousin appeared on the Moon, running. He didn't seem frightened, or even amazed: he placed his hands on the terrain, flinging himself into his usual somersault, but this time after he had hurled himself into the air he remained suspended, as little Xlthlx had. He hovered a moment between Moon and Earth, upside down, then laboriously moving his arms, like someone swimming against a current, he headed with unusual slowness toward our planet.

From the Moon the other sailors hastened to follow his example. Nobody gave a thought to getting the Moon-milk that had been collected into the boats, nor did the Captain scold them for this. They had already waited too long, the distance was difficult to cross by now; when they tried to imitate my cousin's leap or his swimming, they remained there groping, suspended in midair. "Cling together! Idiots! Cling together!" the Captain yelled. At this command, the sailors tried to form a group, a mass, to push all together until they reached the zone of the Earth's attraction: all of a sudden a cascade of bodies plunged into the sea with a loud splash.

The boats were now rowing to pick them up. "Wait! The Captain's wife is missing!" I shouted. The Captain's wife had also tried to jump, but she was still floating only a few yards from the Moon, slowly moving her long, silvery arms in the air. I climbed up the ladder, and in a vain attempt to give her something to grasp I held the harp out toward her. "I can't reach her! We have to go after her!" and I started to jump up, brandishing the harp. Above me the enormous lunar disk no longer seemed the same as before: it had become much smaller, it kept contracting, as if my gaze were driving it away, and the emptied sky gaped like an abyss where, at the bottom, the stars had begun multiplying, and the night poured a river of emptiness over me, drowned me in dizziness and alarm.

"I'm afraid," I thought. "I'm too afraid to jump. I'm a coward!" and at that moment I jumped. I swam furiously through the sky, and held the harp out to her, and instead of coming toward me she rolled over and over, showing me first her impassive face and then her backside.

"Hold tight to me!" I shouted, and I was already overtaking her, entwining my limbs with hers. "If we cling together we can go down!" and I was concentrating all my strength on uniting myself more closely with her, and I concentrated my sensations as I enjoyed the fullness of that embrace. I was so absorbed I didn't realize at first that I was, indeed, tearing her from her weightless condition, but was making her fall back on the Moon. Didn't I realize it? Or had that been my intention from the very beginning? Before I could think properly, a cry was already bursting from my throat. "I'll be the one to stay with you for a month!" Or rather, "On you!" I shouted, in my excitement: "On you for a month!" and at that moment our embrace was broken by our fall to the Moon's surface, where we rolled away from each other among those cold scales.

I raised my eyes as I did every time I touched the Moon's crust, sure that I would see above me the native sea like an endless ceiling, and I saw it, yes, I saw it this time, too, but much higher, and much more narrow, bound by its borders of coasts and cliffs and promontories, and how small the boats seemed, and how unfamiliar my friends' faces and how weak their cries! A sound reached me from nearby: Mrs. Vhd Vhd had discovered her harp and was caressing it, sketching out a chord as sad as weeping.

A long month began. The Moon turned slowly around the Earth. On the suspended globe we no longer saw our familiar shore, but the passage of oceans as deep as abysses and deserts of glowing lapilli, and continents of ice, and forests writhing with reptiles, and the rocky walls of mountain chains gashed by swift rivers, and swampy cities, and stone graveyards, and empires of clay and mud. The distance spread a uniform color over everything: the alien perspectives made every image alien; herds of elephants and swarms of locusts ran over the plains, so evenly vast and dense and thickly grown that there was no difference among them.

I should have been happy: as I had dreamed, I was alone with her, that intimacy with the Moon I had so often envied my cousin and with Mrs. Vhd Vhd was now my exclusive prerogative, a month of days and lunar nights stretched uninterrupted before us, the crust of the satellite nourished us with its milk, whose tart flavor was familiar to us, we raised our eyes up, up to the world where we had been born, finally traversed in all its various expanse, explored landscapes no

13

Earth-being had ever seen, or else we contemplated the stars beyond the Moon, big as pieces of fruit, made of light, ripened on the curved branches of the sky, and everything exceeded my most luminous hopes, and yet, and yet, it was, instead, exile.

I thought only of the Earth. It was the Earth that caused each of us to be that someone he was rather than someone else; up there, wrested from the Earth, it was as if I were no longer that I, nor she that She, for me. I was eager to return to the Earth, and I trembled at the fear of having lost it. The fulfillment of my dream of love had lasted only that instant when we had been united, spinning between Earth and Moon; torn from its earthly soil, my love now knew only the heart-rending nostalgia for what it lacked: a where, a surrounding, a before, an after.

This is what I was feeling. But she? As I asked myself, I was torn by my fears. Because if she also thought only of the Earth, this could be a good sign, a sign that she had finally come to understand me, but it could also mean that everything had been useless, that her longings were directed still and only toward my deaf cousin. Instead, she felt nothing. She never raised her eyes to the old planet, she went off, pale, among those wastelands, mumbling dirges and stroking her harp, as if completely identified with her temporary (as I thought) lunar state. Did this mean I had won out over my rival? No; I had lost: a hopeless defeat. Because she had finally realized that my cousin loved only the Moon, and the only thing she wanted now was to become the Moon, to be assimilated into the object of that extrahuman love.

When the Moon had completed its circling of the planet, there we were again over the Zinc Cliffs. I recognized them with dismay: not even in my darkest previsions had I thought the distance would have made them so tiny. In that mud puddle of the sea, my friends had set forth again, without the now useless ladders; but from the boats rose a kind of forest of long poles; everybody was brandishing one, with a harpoon or a grappling hook at the end, perhaps in the hope of scraping off a last bit of Moon-milk or of lending some kind of help to us

14

wretches up there. But it was soon clear that no pole was long enough to reach the Moon; and they dropped back, ridiculously short, humbled, floating on the sea; and in that confusion some of the boats were thrown off balance and overturned. But just then, from another vessel a longer pole, which till then they had dragged along on the water's surface, began to rise: it must have been made of bamboo, of many, many bamboo poles stuck one into the other, and to raise it they had to go slowly because—thin as it was—if they let it sway too much it might break. Therefore, they had to use it with great strength and skill, so that the wholly vertical weight wouldn't rock the boat.

Suddenly it was clear that the tip of that pole would touch the Moon, and we saw it graze, then press against the scaly terrain, rest there a moment, give a kind of little push, or rather a strong push that made it bounce off again, then come back and strike that same spot as if on the rebound, then move away once more. And I recognized, we both—the Captain's wife and I—recognized my cousin: it couldn't have been anyone else, he was playing his last game with the Moon, one of his tricks, with the Moon on the tip of his pole as if he were juggling with her. And we realized that his virtuosity had no purpose, aimed at no practical result, indeed you would have said he was driving the Moon away, that he was helping her departure, that he wanted to show her to her more distant orbit. And this, too, was just like him: he was unable to conceive desires that went against the Moon's nature, the Moon's course and destiny, and if the Moon now tended to go away from him, then he would take delight in this separation just as, till now, he had delighted in the Moon's nearness.

What could Mrs. Vhd Vhd do, in the face of this? It was only at this moment that she proved her passion for the deaf man hadn't been a frivolous whim but an irrevocable vow. If what my cousin now loved was the distant Moon, then she too would remain distant, on the Moon. I sensed this, seeing that she didn't take a step toward the bamboo pole, but simply turned her harp toward the Earth, high in the sky, and plucked

15

the strings. I say I saw her, but to tell the truth I only caught a glimpse of her out of the corner of my eye, because the minute the pole had touched the lunar crust, I had sprung and grasped it, and now, fast as a snake, I was climbing up the bamboo knots, pushing myself along with jerks of my arms and knees, light in the rarefied space, driven by a natural power that ordered me to return to the Earth, oblivious of the motive that had brought me here, or perhaps more aware of it than ever and of its unfortunate outcome; and already my climb up the swaying pole had reached the point where I no longer had to make any effort but could just allow myself to slide, head-first, attracted by the Earth, until in my haste the pole broke into a thousand pieces and I fell into the sea, among the boats.

My return was sweet, my home refound, but my thoughts were filled only with grief at having lost her, and my eyes gazed at the Moon, forever beyond my reach, as I sought her. And I saw her. She was there where I had left her, lying on a beach directly over our heads, and she said nothing. She was the color of the Moon; she held the harp at her side and moved one hand now and then in slow arpeggios. I could distinguish the shape of her bosom, her arms, her thighs, just as I remember them now, just as now, when the Moon has become that flat, remote circle, I still look for her as soon as the first sliver appears in the sky, and the more it waxes, the more clearly I imagine I can see her, her or something of her, but only her, in a hundred, a thousand different vistas, she who makes the Moon the Moon and, whenever she is full, sets the dogs to howling all night long, and me with them.

AT DAYBREAK

*The planets of the solar system,
G. P. Kuiper explains, began to solidify in the darkness, through
the condensation of a fluid, shapeless nebula. All was cold and
dark. Later the Sun began to become more concentrated until
it was reduced almost to its present dimensions, and in this
process the temperature rose and rose, to thousands of degrees,
and the Sun started emitting radiations in space.*

Pitch-dark it was,—*old Qfwfq confirmed,*—I was only a child,
I can barely remember it. We were there, as usual, with Father
and Mother, Granny Bb'b, some uncles and aunts who were
visiting, Mr. Hnw, the one who later became a horse, and us
little ones. I think I've told you before the way we lived on
the nebulae: it was like lying down, we were flat and very still,
turning as they turned. Not that we were lying outside, you
understand, on the nebula's surface; no, it was too cold out
there. We were underneath, as if we had been tucked in under
a layer of fluid, grainy matter. There was no way of telling time;
whenever we started counting the nebula's turns there were
disagreements, because we didn't have any reference points in
the darkness, and we ended up arguing. So we preferred to let
the centuries flow by as if they were minutes; there was nothing
to do but wait, keep covered as best we could, doze, speak out
now and then to make sure we were all still there; and, naturally, scratch ourselves; because—they can say what they like—
all those particles spinning around had only one effect, a trouble-
some itching.

What we were waiting for, nobody could have said; to be
sure, Granny Bb'b remembered back to the times when matter
was uniformly scattered in space, and there was heat and light;
even allowing for all the exaggerations there must have been in
those old folks' tales, those times had surely been better in some

19

ways, or at least different; but as far as we were concerned, we just had to get through that enormous night.

My sister G'd(w)n fared the best, thanks to her introverted nature: she was a shy girl and she loved the dark. For herself, G'd(w)n always chose to stay in places that were a bit removed, at the edge of the nebula, and she would contemplate the blackness, and toy with the little grains of dust in tiny cascades, and talk to herself, with faint bursts of laughter that were like tiny cascades of dust, and—waking or sleeping—she abandoned herself to dreams. They weren't dreams like ours (in the midst of the darkness, we dreamed of more darkness, because nothing else came into our minds); no, she dreamed—from what we could understand of her ravings—of a darkness a hundred times deeper and more various and velvety.

My father was the first to notice something was changing. I had dozed off, when his shout wakened me: "Watch out! We're hitting something!"

Beneath us, the nebula's matter, instead of fluid as it had always been, was beginning to condense.

To tell the truth, my mother had been tossing and turning for several hours, saying: "Uff, I just can't seem to make myself comfortable here!" In other words, according to her, she had become aware of a change in the place where she was lying: the dust wasn't the same as it had been before, soft, elastic, uniform, so you could wallow in it as much as you liked without leaving any print; instead, a kind of rut or furrow was being formed, especially where she was accustomed to resting all her weight. And she thought she could feel underneath her something like granules or blobs or bumps; which perhaps, after all, were buried hundreds of miles farther down and were pressing through all those layers of soft dust. Not that we generally paid much attention to these premonitions of my mother's: poor thing, for a hypersensitive creature like herself, and already well along in years, our way of life then was hardly ideal for the nerves.

And then it was my brother Rwzfs, an infant at the time; at a certain point I felt him—who knows?—slamming or digging or writhing in some way, and I asked: "What are you doing?" And he said: "I'm playing."

"Playing? With what?"

"With a thing," he said.

You understand? It was the first time. There had never been things to play with before. And how could we have played? With that pap of gaseous matter? Some fun: that sort of stuff was all right perhaps for my sister $G'd(w)^n$. If Rwzfs was playing, it meant he had found something new: in fact, afterwards, exaggerating as usual, they said he had found a pebble. It wasn't a pebble, but it was surely a collection of more solid matter or—let's say—something less gaseous. He was never very clear on this point; that is, he told stories, as they occurred to him, and when the period came when nickel was formed and nobody talked of anything but nickel, he said: "That's it: it was nickel. I was playing with some nickel!" So afterwards he was always called "Nickel Rwzfs." (It wasn't, as some say now, that he had turned into nickel, unable—retarded as he was—to go beyond the mineral phase; it was a different thing altogether, and I only mention this out of love for truth, not because he was my brother: he had always been a bit backward, true enough, but not of the metallic type, if anything a bit colloidal; in fact, when he was still very young, he married an alga, one of the first, and we never heard from him again.)

In short, it seemed everyone had felt something: except me. Maybe it's because I'm absent-minded. I heard—I don't know whether awake or asleep—our father's cry: "We're hitting something!," a meaningless expression (since before then nothing had ever hit anything, you can be sure), but one that took on meaning at the very moment it was uttered, that is, it meant the sensation we were beginning to experience, slightly nauseating, like a slab of mud passing under us, something flat, on which we felt we were bouncing. And I said, in a reproachful tone: "Oh, Granny!"

Afterwards I often asked myself why my first reaction was to become angry with our grandmother. Granny Bb'b, who clung to her habits of the old days, often did embarrassing

21

things: she continued to believe that matter was in uniform expansion and, for example, that it was enough to throw refuse anywhere and it would rarefy and disappear into the distance. The fact that the process of condensation had begun some while ago, that is, that dirt thickened on particles so we weren't able to get rid of it—she couldn't get this into her head. So in some obscure way I connected this new fact of "hitting" with some mistake my grandmother might have made and I let out that cry.

Then Granny Bb'b answered: "What is it? Have you found my cushion?"

This cushion was a little ellipsoid of galactic matter Granny had found somewhere or other during the first cataclysms of the universe; and she always carried it around with her, to sit on. At a certain point, during the great night, it had been lost, and she accused me of having hidden it from her. Now, it was true I had always hated that cushion, it seemed so vulgar and out of place on our nebula, but the most Granny could blame me for was not having guarded it always as she had wanted me to.

Even my father, who was always very respectful toward her, couldn't help remarking: "Oh see here, Mamma, something is happening—we don't know what—and you go on about that cushion!"

"Ah, I told you I couldn't get to sleep!" my mother said: another remark hardly appropriate to the situation.

At that point we heard a great "Pwack! Wack! Sgrr!" and we realized that something must have happened to Mr. Hnw: he was hawking and spitting for all he was worth.

"Mr. Hnw! Mr. Hnw! Get hold of yourself! Where's he got to now?" my father started saying, and in that darkness, still without a ray of light, we managed to grope until we found him and could hoist him onto the surface of the nebula, where he caught his breath again. We laid him out on that external layer which was then taking on a clotted, slippery consistency.

"Wrrak! This stuff closes on you!" Mr. Hnw tried to say, though he didn't have a great gift for self-expression. "You go down and down, and you swallow! Skrrrack!" He spat.

There was another novelty: if you weren't careful, you could

22

now sink on the nebula. My mother, with a mother's instinct, was the first to realize it. And she cried: "Children: are you all there? Where are you?"

The truth was that we were a bit confused, and whereas before, when everything had been lying regularly for centuries, we were always careful not to scatter, now we had forgotten all about it.

"Keep calm. Nobody must stray," my father said.

"$G'd(w)^n$! Where are you? And the twins? Has anybody seen the twins? Speak up!"

Nobody answered. "Oh, my goodness, they're lost!" Mother shouted. My little brothers weren't yet old enough to know how to transmit any message: so they got lost easily and had to be watched over constantly. "I'll go look for them!" I said.

"Good for you, Qfwfq, yes, go!" Father and Mother said, then, immediately repentant: "But if you do go, you'll be lost, too! No, stay here. Oh, all right, go, but let us know where you are: whistle!"

I began to walk in the darkness, in the marshy condensation of that nebula, emitting a constant whistle. I say "walk"; I mean a way of moving over the surface, inconceivable until a few minutes earlier, and it was already an achievement to attempt it now, because the matter offered such little resistance that, if you weren't careful, instead of proceeding on the surface you sank sideways or even vertically and were buried. But in whatever direction I went and at whatever level, the chances of finding the twins remained the same: who could guess where the two of them had got to?

All of a sudden I sprawled; as if they had—we would say today—tripped me up. It was the first time I had fallen, I didn't know what "to fall" was, but we were still on the softness and I didn't hurt myself. "Don't trample here," a voice said, "I don't want you to, Qfwfq." It was the voice of my sister $G'd(w)^n$.

"Why? What's there?"

"I made some things with things . . ." she said. It took me a while to realize, groping, that my sister, messing about with

23

that sort of mud, had built up a little hill, all full of pinnacles, spires, and battlements.

"What have you done there?"

G'd(w)^n never gave you a straight answer. "An outside with an inside in it."

I continued my walk, falling every now and then. I also stumbled over the inevitable Mr. Hnw, who was stuck in the condensing matter again, head-first. "Come, Mr. Hnw. Mr. Hnw! Can't you possibly stay erect?" and I had to help him pull himself out once more, this time pushing him from below, because I was also completely immersed.

Mr. Hnw, coughing and puffing and sneezing (it had never been so icy cold before), popped up on the surface at the very spot where Granny Bb'b was sitting. Granny flew into the air, immediately overcome with emotion: "My grandchildren! My grandchildren are back!"

"No, no, Mamma. Look, it's Mr. Hnw!" Everything was confused.

"But the grandchildren?"

"They're here!" I shouted, "and the cushion is here, too!"

The twins must long before have made a secret hiding place for themselves in the thickness of the nebula, and they had hidden the cushion there, to play with. As long as matter had been fluid, they could float in there and do somersaults through the round cushion, but now they were imprisoned in a kind of spongy cream: the cushion's central hole was clogged up, and they felt crushed on all sides.

"Hang on to the cushion," I tried to make them understand. "I'll pull you out, you little fools!" I pulled and pulled and, at a certain point, before they knew what was happening, they were already rolling about on the surface, now covered with a scabby film like the white of an egg. The cushion, instead, dissolved as soon as it emerged. There was no use trying to understand the phenomena that took place in those days; and there was no use trying to explain to Granny Bb'b.

Just then, as if they couldn't have chosen a better moment, our visiting relatives got up slowly and said: "Well, it's getting late; I wonder what our children are up to. We're a little worried about them. It's been nice seeing all of you again, but we'd better be getting along."

Nobody could say they were wrong; in fact, they should have taken fright and run off long since; but this couple, perhaps because of the out-of-the-way place where they lived, were a bit gauche. Perhaps they had been on pins and needles all this time and hadn't dared say so.

My father said: "Well, if you want to go, I won't try to keep you. But think it over: maybe it would be wiser to stay until the situation's cleared up a bit, because as things stand now, you don't know what sort of risk you might be running." Good, common sense, in short.

But they insisted: "No, no, thanks all the same. It's been a real nice get-together, but we won't intrude on you any longer," and more nonsense of the sort. In other words, we may not have understood very much of the situation, but they had no notion of it at all.

There were three of them: an aunt and two uncles, all three very tall and practically identical; we never really understood which uncle was the husband and which the brother, or exactly how they were related to us: in those days there were many things that were left vague.

They began to go off, one at a time, each in a different direction, toward the black sky, and every now and then, as if to maintain contact, they cried: "Oh! Oh!" They always acted like this: they weren't capable of behaving with any sort of system.

They had hardly left when their cries of "Oh! Oh!" could be heard from very distant points, though they ought to have been still only a few paces away. And we could also hear some exclamations of theirs, whose meaning we couldn't understand: "Why, it's hollow here!" "You can't get past this spot!" "Then why don't you come here?" "Where are you?" "Jump!" "Fine! And what do I jump over?" "Oh, but now we're heading back again!" In other words, everything was incomprehensible, except the fact that some enormous distances were stretching out between us and those relatives.

It was our aunt, the last to leave, whose yells made the most sense: "Here I am, all alone, stuck on top of a piece of this stuff that's come loose . . ."

And the voices of the two uncles, weak now in the distance, repeated: "Fool . . . Fool . . . Fool . . ."

We were peering into this darkness, crisscrossed with voices, when the change took place: the only real, great change I've ever happened to witness, and compared to it the rest is nothing. I mean this thing that began at the horizon, this vibration which didn't resemble those we then called sounds, or those now called the "hitting" vibrations, or any others; a kind of eruption, distant surely, and yet, at the same time, it made what was close come closer; in other words, all the darkness was suddenly dark in contrast with something else that wasn't darkness, namely light. As soon as we could make a more careful analysis of the situation, it turned out that: first, the sky was dark as before but was beginning to be not so dark; second, the surface where we were was all bumpy and crusty, an ice so dirty it was revolting, which was rapidly dissolving because the temperature was rising at full speed; and, third, there was what we would later have called a source of light, that is, a mass that was becoming incandescent, separated from us by an enormous empty space, and it seemed to be trying out all the colors one by one, in iridescent fits and starts. And there was more: in the midst of the sky, between us and that incandescent mass, a couple of islands, brightly lighted and vague, which whirled in the void with our uncles on them and other people, reduced to distant shadows, letting out a kind of chirping noise.

So the better part was done: the heart of the nebula, contracting, had developed warmth and light, and now there was the Sun. All the rest went on revolving nearby, divided and clotted into various pieces, Mercury, Venus, the Earth, and others farther on, and whoever was on them, stayed where he was. And, above all, it was deathly hot.

We stood there, open-mouthed, erect, except for Mr. Hnw who was on all fours, to be on the safe side. And my grandmother! How she laughed! As I said before, Granny Bb'b dated from the age of diffused luminosity, and all through this

26

dark time she had kept saying that any minute things would go back the way they had been in the old days. Now her moment seemed to have come; for a while she tried to act casual, the sort of person who accepts anything that happens as perfectly natural; then, seeing we paid her no attention, she started laughing and calling us: "Bunch of ignorant louts . . . Know-nothings . . ."

She wasn't speaking quite in good faith, however; unless her memory by then had begun to fail her. My father, understanding what little he did, said to her, prudently as always: "Mamma, I know what you mean, but really, this seems quite a different phenomenon . . ." And he pointed to the terrain: "Look down!" he exclaimed.

We lowered our eyes. The Earth which supported us was still a gelatinous, diaphanous mass, growing more and more firm and opaque, beginning from the center where a kind of yolk was thickening; but still our eyes managed to penetrate through it, illuminated as it was by that first Sun. And in the midst of this kind of transparent bubble we saw a shadow moving, as if swimming and flying. And our mother said: "Daughter!"

We all recognized G'd(w)[n]: frightened perhaps by the Sun's catching fire, following a reaction of her shy spirit, she had sunk into the condensing matter of the Earth, and now she was trying to clear a path for herself in the depths of the planet, and she looked like a gold and silver butterfly as she passed into a zone that was still illuminated and diaphanous or vanished into the sphere of shadow that was growing wider and wider.

"G'd(w)[n]! G'd(w)[n]!" we shouted and flung ourselves on the ground, also trying to clear a way, to reach her. But the Earth's surface now was coagulating more and more into a porous husk, and my brother Rwzfs, who had managed to stick his head into a fissure, was almost strangled.

Then she was seen no more: the solid zone now occupied the whole central part of the planet. My sister had remained in there, and I never found out whether she had stayed buried in those depths or whether she had reached safety on the other

27

side until I met her, much later, at Canberra in 1912, married to a certain Sullivan, a retired railroad man, so changed I hardly recognized her.

We got up. Mr. Hnw and Granny were in front of us, crying, surrounded by pale blue-and-gold flames.

"Rwzfs! Why have you set fire to Granny?" Father began to scold, but, turning toward my brother, he saw that Rwzfs was also enveloped in flames. And so was my father, and my mother, too, and I—we were all burning in the fire. Or rather: we weren't burning, we were immersed in it as in a dazzling forest; the flames shot high over the whole surface of the planet, a fiery air in which we could run and float and fly, and we were gripped by a kind of new joy.

The Sun's radiations were burning the envelopes of the planets, made of helium and hydrogen: in the sky, where our uncles and aunt were, fiery globes spun, dragging after them long beards of gold and turquoise, as a comet drags its tail.

The darkness came back. By now we were sure that everything that could possibly happen had happened, and "yes, this is the end," Grandmother said, "mind what us old folks say . . ." Instead, the Earth had merely made one of its turns. It was night. Everything was just beginning.

A SIGN
IN SPACE

Situated in the external zone of the Milky Way, the Sun takes about two hundred million years to make a complete revolution of the Galaxy.

Right, that's how long it takes, not a day less,—*Qfwfq said,*—once, as I went past, I drew a sign at a point in space, just so I could find it again two hundred million years later, when we went by the next time around. What sort of sign? It's hard to explain because if I say sign to you, you immediately think of a something that can be distinguished from a something else, but nothing could be distinguished from anything there; you immediately think of a sign made with some implement or with your hands, and then when you take the implement or your hands away, the sign remains, but in those days there were no implements or even hands, or teeth, or noses, all things that came along afterwards, a long time afterwards. As to the form a sign should have, you say it's no problem because, whatever form it may be given, a sign only has to serve as a sign, that is, be different or else the same as other signs: here again it's easy for you young ones to talk, but in that period I didn't have any examples to follow, I couldn't say I'll make it the same or I'll make it different, there were no things to copy, nobody knew what a line was, straight or curved, or even a dot, or a protuberance or a cavity. I conceived the idea of making a sign, that's true enough, or rather, I conceived the idea of considering a sign a something that I felt like making, so when, at that point in space and not in another, I made something, meaning to make a sign, it turned out that I really had made a sign, after all.

In other words, considering it was the first sign ever made in the universe, or at least in the circuit of the Milky Way, I must admit it came out very well. Visible? What a question! Who had eyes to see with in those days? Nothing had ever been

31

seen by anything, the question never even arose. Recognizable, yes, beyond any possibility of error: because all the other points in space were the same, indistinguishable, and instead, this one had the sign on it.

So as the planets continued their revolutions, and the solar system went on in its own, I soon left the sign far behind me, separated from it by the endless fields of space. And I couldn't help thinking about when I would come back and encounter it again, and how I would know it, and how happy it would make me, in that anonymous expanse, after I had spent a hundred thousand light-years without meeting anything familiar, nothing for hundreds of centuries, for thousands of millennia; I'd come back and there it would be in its place, just as I had left it, simple and bare, but with that unmistakable imprint, so to speak, that I had given it.

Slowly the Milky Way revolved, with its fringe of constellations and planets and clouds, and the Sun along with the rest, toward the edge. In all that circling, only the sign remained still, in an ordinary spot, out of all the orbit's reach (to make it, I had leaned over the border of the Galaxy a little, so it would remain outside and all those revolving worlds wouldn't crash into it), in an ordinary point that was no longer ordinary since it was the only point that was surely there, and which could be used as a reference point to distinguish other points.

I thought about it day and night; in fact, I couldn't think about anything else; actually, this was the first opportunity I had had to think something; or I should say: to think something had never been possible, first because there were no things to think about, and second because signs to think of them by were lacking, but from the moment there was that sign, it was possible for someone thinking to think of a sign, and therefore that one, in the sense that the sign was the thing you could think about and also the sign of the thing thought, namely, itself.

So the situation was this: the sign served to mark a place but at the same time it meant that in that place there was a sign (something far more important because there were plenty of places but there was only one sign) and also at the same time

32

that sign was mine, the sign of me, because it was the only sign I had ever made and I was the only one who had ever made signs. It was like a name, the name of that point, and also my name that I had signed on that spot; in short, it was the only name available for everything that required a name.

Transported by the sides of the Galaxy, our world went navigating through distant spaces, and the sign stayed where I had left it to mark that spot, and at the same time it marked me, I carried it with me, it inhabited me, possessed me entirely, came between me and everything with which I might have attempted to establish a relationship. As I waited to come back and meet it again, I could try to derive other signs from it and combinations of signs, series of similar signs and contrasts of different signs. But already tens and tens of thousands of millennia had gone by since the moment when I had made it (rather, since the few seconds in which I had scrawled it down in the constant movement of the Milky Way) and now, just when I needed to bear in mind its every detail (the slightest uncertainty about its form made uncertain the possible distinctions between it and other signs I might make), I realized that, though I recalled its general outline, its over-all appearance, still something about it eluded me, I mean if I tried to break it down into its various elements, I couldn't remember whether, between one part and the other, it went like this or like that. I needed it there in front of me, to study, to consult, but instead it was still far away, I didn't yet know how far, because I had made it precisely in order to know the time it would take me to see it again, and until I had found it once more, I wouldn't know. Now, however, it wasn't my motive in making it that mattered to me, but how it was made, and I started inventing hypotheses about this how, and theories according to which a certain sign had to be perforce in a certain way, or else, proceeding by exclusion, I tried to eliminate all the less probable types of sign to arrive at the right one, but all these imaginary signs vanished inevitably because that first sign was missing as a term of comparison. As I racked my brain like this (while the Galaxy went on turning wakefully in its bed of soft

33

emptiness and the atoms burned and radiated) I realized I had lost by now even that confused notion of my sign, and I succeeded in conceiving only interchangeable fragments of signs, that is, smaller signs within the large one, and every change of these signs-within-the-sign changed the sign itself into a completely different one; in short, I had completely forgotten what my sign was like and, try as I might, it wouldn't come back to my mind.

Did I despair? No, this forgetfulness was annoying, but not irreparable. Whatever happened, I knew the sign was there waiting for me, quiet and still. I would arrive, I would find it again, and I would then be able to pick up the thread of my meditations. At a rough guess, I calculated we had completed half of our galactic revolution: I had only to be patient, the second half always seemed to go by more quickly. Now I just had to remember the sign existed and I would pass it again.

Day followed day, and then I knew I must be near. I was furiously impatient because I might encounter the sign at any moment. It's here, no, a little farther on, now I'll count up to a hundred . . . Had it disappeared? Had we already gone past it? I didn't know. My sign had perhaps remained who knows where, behind, completely remote from the revolutionary orbit of our system. I hadn't calculated the oscillations to which, especially in those days, the celestial bodies' fields of gravity were subject, and which caused them to trace irregular orbits, cut like the flower of a dahlia. For about a hundred millennia I tormented myself, going over my calculations: it turned out that our course touched that spot not every galactic year but only every three, that is, every six hundred million solar years. When you've waited two hundred million years, you can also wait six hundred; and I waited; the way was long but I wasn't on foot, after all; astride the Galaxy I traveled through the light-years, galloping over the planetary and stellar orbits as if I were on a horse whose shoes struck sparks; I was in a state of mounting excitement; I felt I was going forth to conquer the only thing that mattered to me, sign and dominion and name . . .

I made the second circuit, the third. I was there. I let out a yell. At a point which had to be that very point, in the place of my sign, there was a shapeless scratch, a bruised, chipped abrasion of space. I had lost everything: the sign, the point, the thing that caused me—being the one who had made the sign at that point—to be me. Space, without a sign, was once again a chasm, the void, without beginning or end, nauseating, in which everything—including me—was lost. (And don't come telling me that, to fix a point, my sign and the erasure of my sign amounted to the same thing; the erasure was the negation of the sign, and therefore didn't serve to distinguish one point from the preceding and successive points.)

I was disheartened and for many light-years I let myself be dragged along as if I were unconscious. When I finally raised my eyes (in the meanwhile, sight had begun in our world, and, as a result, also life), I saw what I would never have expected to see. I saw it, the sign, but not that one, a similar sign, a sign unquestionably copied from mine, but one I realized immediately couldn't be mine, it was so squat and careless and clumsily pretentious, a wretched counterfeit of what I had meant to indicate with that sign whose ineffable purity I could only now—through contrast—recapture. Who had played this trick on me? I couldn't figure it out. Finally, a plurimillennial chain of deductions led me to the solution: on another planetary system which performed its galactic revolution before us, there was a certain Kgwgk (the name I deduced afterwards, in the later era of names), a spiteful type, consumed with envy, who had erased my sign in a vandalistic impulse and then, with vulgar artifice, had attempted to make another.

It was clear that his sign had nothing to mark except Kgwgk's intention to imitate my sign, which was beyond all comparison. But at that moment the determination not to let my rival get the better of me was stronger than any other desire: I wanted immediately to make a new sign in space, a real sign that would make Kgwgk die of envy. About seven hundred millions of years had gone by since I had first tried to make a sign, but I fell to work with a will. Now things were different, however, because the world, as I mentioned, was beginning to produce an image of itself, and in everything a form was beginning to correspond to a function, and the forms of that time, we believed, had a long future ahead of them (instead, we were wrong: take—to give you a fairly recent example—the dinosaurs), and therefore in this new sign of mine you could perceive the influence of our new way of looking at things, call it style if you like, that special way that everything had to be, there, in a certain fashion. I must say I was truly satisfied with it, and I no longer regretted that first sign that had been erased, because this one seemed vastly more beautiful to me.

But in the duration of that galactic year we already began to realize that the world's forms had been temporary up until then, and that they would change, one by one. And this awareness was accompanied by a certain annoyance with the old images, so that even their memory was intolerable. I began to be tormented by a thought: I had left that sign in space, that sign which had seemed so beautiful and original to me and so suited to its function, and which now, in my memory, seemed inappropriate, in all its pretension, a sign chiefly of an antiquated way of conceiving signs and of my foolish acceptance of an order of things I ought to have been wise enough to break away from in time. In other words, I was ashamed of that sign which went on through the centuries, being passed by worlds in flight, making a ridiculous spectacle of itself and of me and of that temporary way we had had of seeing things. I blushed when I remembered it (and I remembered it constantly), blushes that lasted whole geological eras: to hide my shame I crawled into the craters of the volcanoes, in remorse I sank my teeth into the caps of the glaciations that covered the continents. I was tortured by the thought that Kgwgk, always preceding me in the circumnavigation of the Milky Way, would see the sign before I could erase it, and boor that he was, he would mock me and make fun of me, contemptuously repeating the sign in rough caricatures in every corner of the circumgalactic sphere.

Instead, this time the complicated astral timekeeping was

in my favor. Kgwgk's constellation didn't encounter the sign, whereas our solar system turned up there punctually at the end of the first revolution, so close that I was able to erase the whole thing with the greatest care.

Now, there wasn't a single sign of mine in space. I could start drawing another, but I knew that signs also allow others to judge the one who makes them, and that in the course of a galactic year tastes and ideas have time to change, and the way of regarding the earlier ones depends on what comes afterwards; in short, I was afraid a sign that now might seem perfect to me, in two hundred or six hundred million years would make me look absurd. Instead, in my nostalgia, the first sign, brutally rubbed out by Kgwgk, remained beyond the attacks of time and its changes, the sign created before the beginning of forms, which was to contain something that would have survived all forms, namely the fact of being a sign and nothing else.

Making signs that weren't that sign no longer held any interest for me; and I had forgotten that sign now, billions of years before. So, unable to make true signs, but wanting somehow to annoy Kgwgk, I started making false signs, notches in space, holes, stains, little tricks that only an incompetent creature like Kgwgk could mistake for signs. And still he furiously got rid of them with his erasings (as I could see in later revolutions), with a determination that must have cost him much effort. (Now I scattered these false signs liberally through space, to see how far his simple-mindedness would go.)

Observing these erasures, one circuit after the next (the Galaxy's revolutions had now become for me a slow, boring voyage without goal or expectation), I realized something: as the galactic years passed the erasures tended to fade in space, and beneath them what I had drawn at those points, my false signs—as I called them—began to reappear. This discovery, far from displeasing me, filled me with new hope. If Kgwgk's erasures were erased, the first he had made, there at that point, must have disappeared by now, and my sign must have returned to its pristine visibility!

So expectation was revived, to lend anxiety to my days. The

Galaxy turned like an omelet in its heated pan, itself both frying pan and golden egg; and I was frying, with it, in my impatience.

But, with the passing of the galactic years, space was no longer that uniformly barren and colorless expanse. The idea of fixing with signs the points where we passed—as it had come to me and to Kgwgk—had occurred to many, scattered over billions of planets of other solar systems, and I was constantly running into one of these things, or a pair, or even a dozen, simple two-dimensional scrawls, or else three-dimensional solids (polyhedrons, for example), or even things constructed with more care, with the fourth dimension and everything. So it happened that I reached the point of my sign, and I found five, all there. And I wasn't able to recognize my own. It's this one, no, that; no, no, that one seems too modern, but it could also be the most ancient; I don't recognize my hand in that one, I would never have wanted to make it like that . . . And meanwhile the Galaxy ran through space and left behind those signs old and new and I still hadn't found mine.

I'm not exaggerating when I say that the galactic years that followed were the worst I had ever lived through. I went on looking, and signs kept growing thicker in space; from all the worlds anybody who had an opportunity invariably left his mark in space somehow; and our world, too, every time I turned, I found more crowded, so that world and space seemed the mirror of each other, both minutely adorned with hieroglyphics and ideograms, each of which might be a sign and might not be: a calcareous concretion on basalt, a crest raised by the wind on the clotted sand of the desert, the arrangement of the eyes in a peacock's tail (gradually, living among signs had led us to see signs in countless things that, before, were there, marking nothing but their own presence; they had been transformed into the sign of themselves and had been added to the series of signs made on purpose by those who meant to make a sign), the fire-streaks against a wall of schistose rock, the four-hundred-and-twenty-seventh groove—slightly crooked—of the cornice of a tomb's pediment, a sequence of streaks on a video during a thunderstorm (the series of signs was multiplied in the series of the signs of signs, of signs repeated countless times always the same and always somehow different because to the purposely made sign you had to add the sign that had happened there by chance), the badly inked tail of the letter R in an evening newspaper joined to a thready imperfection in the paper, one among the eight hundred thousand flakings of a tarred wall in the Melbourne docks, the curve of a graph, a skid-mark on the asphalt, a chromosome . . . Every now and then I'd start: that's the one! And for a second I was sure I had rediscovered my sign, on the Earth or in space, it made no difference, because through the signs a continuity had been established with no precise boundaries any more.

In the universe now there was no longer a container and a thing contained, but only a general thickness of signs superimposed and coagulated, occupying the whole volume of space; it was constantly being dotted, minutely, a network of lines and scratches and reliefs and engravings; the universe was scrawled over on all sides, along all its dimensions. There was no longer any way to establish a point of reference: the Galaxy went on turning but I could no longer count the revolutions, any point could be the point of departure, any sign heaped up with the others could be mine, but discovering it would have served no purpose, because it was clear that, independent of signs, space didn't exist and perhaps had never existed.

ALL AT ONE POINT

T*hrough the calculations begun by Edwin P. Hubble on the galaxies' velocity of recession, we can establish the moment when all the universe's matter was concentrated in a single point, before it began to expand in space.*

Naturally, we were all there,—*old Qfwfq said,*—where else could we have been? Nobody knew then that there could be space. Or time either: what use did we have for time, packed in there like sardines?

I say "packed like sardines," using a literary image: in reality there wasn't even space to pack us into. Every point of each of us coincided with every point of each of the others in a single point, which was where we all were. In fact, we didn't even bother one another, except for personality differences, because when space doesn't exist, having somebody unpleasant like Mr. Pber^t Pber^d underfoot all the time is the most irritating thing.

How many of us were there? Oh, I was never able to figure that out, not even approximately. To make a count, we would have had to move apart, at least a little, and instead we all occupied that same point. Contrary to what you might think, it wasn't the sort of situation that encourages sociability; I know, for example, that in other periods neighbors called on one another; but there, because of the fact that we were all neighbors, nobody even said good morning or good evening to anybody else.

In the end each of us associated only with a limited number of acquaintances. The ones I remember most are Mrs. Ph(i)Nk$_o$, her friend De XuaeauX, a family of immigrants by the name of Z'zu, and Mr. Pber^t Pber^d, whom I just mentioned. There was also a cleaning woman—"maintenance staff" she was called

—only one, for the whole universe, since there was so little room. To tell the truth, she had nothing to do all day long, not even dusting—inside one point not even a grain of dust can enter—so she spent all her time gossiping and complaining.

Just with the people I've already named we would have been overcrowded; but you have to add all the stuff we had to keep piled up in there: all the material that was to serve afterwards to form the universe, now dismantled and concentrated in such a way that you weren't able to tell what was later to become part of astronomy (like the nebula of Andromeda) from what was assigned to geography (the Vosges, for example) or to chemistry (like certain beryllium isotopes). And on top of that, we were always bumping against the Z'zu family's household goods: camp beds, mattresses, baskets; these Z'zus, if you weren't careful, with the excuse that they were a large family, would begin to act as if they were the only ones in the world: they even wanted to hang lines across our point to dry their washing.

But the others also had wronged the Z'zus, to begin with, by calling them "immigrants," on the pretext that, since the others had been there first, the Z'zus had come later. This was mere unfounded prejudice—that seems obvious to me—because neither before nor after existed, nor any place to immigrate from, but there were those who insisted that the concept of "immigrant" could be understood in the abstract, outside of space and time.

It was what you might call a narrow-minded attitude, our outlook at that time, very petty. The fault of the environment in which we had been reared. An attitude that, basically, has remained in all of us, mind you: it keeps cropping up even today, if two of us happen to meet—at the bus stop, in a movie house, at an international dentists' convention—and start reminiscing about the old days. We say hello—at times somebody recognizes me, at other times I recognize somebody—and we promptly start asking about this one and that one (even if each remembers only a few of those remembered by the others), and so we start in again on the old disputes, the slanders, the

44

denigrations. Until somebody mentions Mrs. $Ph(i)Nk_0$—every conversation finally gets around to her—and then, all of a sudden, the pettiness is put aside, and we feel uplifted, filled with a blissful, generous emotion. Mrs. $Ph(i)Nk_0$, the only one that none of us has forgotten and that we all regret. Where has she ended up? I have long since stopped looking for her: Mrs. $Ph(i)Nk_0$, her bosom, her thighs, her orange dressing gown—we'll never meet her again, in this system of galaxies or in any other.

Let me make one thing clear: this theory that the universe, after having reached an extremity of rarefaction, will be condensed again has never convinced me. And yet many of us are counting only on that, continually making plans for the time when we'll all be back there again. Last month, I went into the bar here on the corner and whom did I see? Mr. $Pber^t Pber^d$. "What's new with you? How do you happen to be in this neighborhood?" I learned that he's the agent for a plastics firm, in Pavia. He's the same as ever, with his silver tooth, his loud suspenders. "When we go back there," he said to me, in a whisper, "the thing we have to make sure of is, this time, certain people remain out . . . You know who I mean: those Z'zus . . ."

I would have liked to answer him by saying that I've heard a number of people make the same remark, concluding: "You know who I mean . . . Mr. $Pber^t Pber^d$ . . ."

To avoid the subject, I hastened to say: "What about Mrs. $Ph(i)Nk_0$? Do you think we'll find her back there again?"

"Ah, yes . . . She, by all means . . ." he said, turning purple.

For all of us the hope of returning to that point means, above all, the hope of being once more with Mrs. $Ph(i)Nk_0$. (This applies even to me, though I don't believe in it.) And in that bar, as always happens, we fell to talking about her, and were moved; even Mr. $Pber^t Pber^d$'s unpleasantness faded, in the face of that memory.

Mrs. $Ph(i)Nk_0$'s great secret is that she never aroused any jealousy among us. Or any gossip, either. The fact that she went to bed with her friend, Mr. De XuaeauX, was well known. But in a point, if there's a bed, it takes up the whole point, so it isn't a question of *going* to bed, but of *being* there, because anybody in the point is also in the bed. Consequently, it was inevitable that she should be in bed also with each of us. If she had been another person, there's no telling all the things that would have been said about her. It was the cleaning woman who always started the slander, and the others didn't have to be coaxed to imitate her. On the subject of the Z'zu family— for a change!—the horrible things we had to hear: father, daughters, brothers, sisters, mother, aunts: nobody showed any hesitation even before the most sinister insinuation. But with her it was different: the happiness I derived from her was the joy of being concealed, punctiform, in her, and of protecting her, punctiform, in me; it was at the same time vicious contemplation (thanks to the promiscuity of the punctiform convergence of us all in her) and also chastity (given her punctiform impenetrability). In short: what more could I ask?

And all of this, which was true of me, was true also for each of the others. And for her: she contained and was contained with equal happiness, and she welcomed us and loved and inhabited all equally.

We got along so well all together, so well that something extraordinary was bound to happen. It was enough for her to say, at a certain moment: "Oh, if I only had some room, how I'd like to make some noodles for you boys!" And in that moment we all thought of the space that her round arms would occupy, moving backward and forward with the rolling pin over the dough, her bosom leaning over the great mound of flour and eggs which cluttered the wide board while her arms kneaded and kneaded, white and shiny with oil up to the elbows; we thought of the space that the flour would occupy, and the wheat for the flour, and the fields to raise the wheat, and the mountains from which the water would flow to irrigate the fields, and the grazing lands for the herds of calves that would give their meat for the sauce; of the space it would take for the Sun to arrive with its rays, to ripen the wheat; of the space for the

46

Sun to condense from the clouds of stellar gases and burn; of
the quantities of stars and galaxies and galactic masses in flight
through space which would be needed to hold suspended every
galaxy, every nebula, every sun, every planet, and at the same
time we thought of it, this space was inevitably being formed,
at the same time that Mrs. $Ph(i)Nk_0$ was uttering those words:
". . . ah, what noodles, boys!" the point that contained her
and all of us was expanding in a halo of distance in light-years
and light-centuries and billions of light-millennia, and we were
being hurled to the four corners of the universe (Mr. $Pber^t$
$Pber^d$ all the way to Pavia), and she, dissolved into I don't
know what kind of energy-light-heat, she, Mrs. $Ph(i)Nk_0$, she
who in the midst of our closed, petty world had been capable of
a generous impulse, "Boys, the noodles I would make for you!,"
a true outburst of general love, initiating at the same moment
the concept of space and, properly speaking, space itself, and
time, and universal gravitation, and the gravitating universe,
making possible billions and billions of suns, and of planets,
and fields of wheat, and Mrs. $Ph(i)Nk_0$s, scattered through the
continents of the planets, kneading with floury, oil-shiny, generous arms, and she lost at that very moment, and we, mourning her loss.

WITHOUT COLORS

B*efore forming its atmosphere and its oceans, the Earth must have resembled a gray ball revolving in space. As the Moon does now; where the ultraviolet rays radiated by the Sun arrive directly, all colors are destroyed, which is why the cliffs of the lunar surface, instead of being colored like Earth's, are of a dead, uniform gray. If the Earth displays a varicolored countenance, it is thanks to the atmosphere, which filters that murderous light.*

A bit monotonous,—*Qfwfq confirmed,*—but restful, all the same. I could go for miles and miles at top speed, the way you can move where there isn't any air about, and all I could see was gray upon gray. No sharp contrasts: the only really white white, if there was any, lay in the center of the Sun and you couldn't even begin to approach it with your eyes; and as far as really black black is concerned, there wasn't even the darkness of night, because all the stars were constantly visible. Uninterrupted horizons opened before me with mountain chains just beginning to emerge, gray mountains, above gray rocky plains; and though I crossed continent after continent I never came to a shore, because oceans and lakes and rivers were still lying underground somewhere or other.

You rarely met anyone in those days: there were so few of us! To survive with that ultraviolet you couldn't be too demanding. Above all the lack of atmosphere asserted itself in many ways, you take meteors for example: they fell like hail from all the points of space, because then we didn't have the stratosphere where nowadays they strike, as if on a roof, and disintegrate. Then there was the silence: no use shouting! Without any air to vibrate, we were all deaf and dumb. The temperature? There was nothing around to retain the Sun's heat: when night fell it was so cold you could freeze stiff. Fortunately, the Earth's

51

crust warmed us from below, with all those molten minerals which were being compressed in the bowels of the planet. The nights were short (like the days: the Earth turned around faster); I slept huddled up to a very warm rock; the dry cold all around was pleasant. In other words, as far as the climate went, to tell you the truth, I wasn't so badly off.

Among the countless indispensable things we had to do without, the absence of colors—as you can imagine—was the least of our problems; even if we had known they existed, we would have considered them an unsuitable luxury. The only drawback was the strain on your eyes when you had to hunt for something or someone, because with everything equally colorless no form could be clearly distinguished from what was behind it or around it. You could barely make out a moving object: a meteor fragment as it rolled, or the serpentine yawning of a seismic chasm, or a lapillus being ejected from a volcano.

That day I was running through a kind of amphitheater of porous, spongy rocks, all pierced with arches beyond which other arches opened; a very uneven terrain where the absence of color was streaked by distinguishable concave shadows. And among the pillars of these colorless arches I saw a kind of colorless flash running swiftly, disappearing, then reappearing farther on: two flattened glows that appeared and disappeared abruptly; I still hadn't realized what they were, but I was already in love and running, in pursuit of the eyes of Ayl.

I went into a sandy wasteland: I proceeded, sinking down among dunes which were always somehow different and yet almost the same. Depending on the point from which you looked at them, the crests of the dunes seemed the outlines of reclining bodies. There you could almost make out the form of an arm folded over a tender breast, with the palm open under a resting cheek; farther on, a young foot with a slender big toe seemed to emerge. As I stopped to observe those possible analogies, a full minute went by before I realized that, before my eyes, I didn't have a sandy ridge but the object of my pursuit.

She was lying, colorless, overcome with sleep, on the colorless sand. I sat down nearby. It was the season—as I know now

52

—when the ultraviolet era was approaching its end on our planet; a way of life about to finish was displaying its supreme peak of beauty. Nothing so beautiful had ever run over the Earth, as the creature I had before my eyes.

Ayl opened her eyes. She saw me. At first I believe she couldn't distinguish me—as had happened to me, with her—from the rest of that sandy world; then she seemed to recognize in me the unknown presence that had pursued her and she was frightened. But in the end she became aware of our common substance and there was a half-timid, half-smiling palpitation in the look she gave me, which caused me to emit a silent whimper of happiness.

I started conversing, all in gestures. "Sand. Not-sand," I said, first pointing to our surroundings, then to the two of us.

She nodded yes, she had understood.

"Rock. Not-rock," I said, to continue that line of reasoning. It was a period in which we didn't have many concepts at our disposal: to indicate what we two were, for example, what we had in common and what was different, was not an easy undertaking.

"I. You-not-I." I tried to explain, with gestures.

She was irked.

"Yes. You-like-me, but only so much," I corrected myself.

She was a bit reassured, but still suspicious.

"I, you, together, run run," I tried to say.

She burst out laughing and ran off.

We ran along the crest of the volcanoes. In the noon grayness Ayl's flying hair and the tongues of flame that rose from the craters were mingled in a wan, identical fluttering of wings.

"Fire. Hair," I said to her. "Fire same hair."

She seemed convinced.

"Not beautiful?" I asked.

"Beautiful," she answered.

The Sun was already sinking into a whitish sunset. On a crag of opaque rocks, the rays, striking sidelong, made some of the rocks shine.

"Stones there not same. Beautiful, eh?" I said.

"No," she answered, and looked away.

"Stones there beautiful, eh?" I insisted, pointing to the shiny gray of the stones.

"No." She refused to look.

"To you, I, stones there!" I offered her.

"No. Stones here!" Ayl answered and grasped a handful of the opaque ones. But I had already run ahead.

I came back with the glistening stones I had collected, but I had to force her to take them.

"Beautiful!" I tried to persuade her.

"No!" she protested, but she looked at them; removed now from the Sun's reflections, they were opaque like the other stones; and only then did she say: "Beautiful!"

Night fell, the first I had spent not embracing a rock, and perhaps for this reason it seemed cruelly shorter to me. The light tended at every moment to erase Ayl, to cast a doubt on her presence, but the darkness restored my certainty she was there.

The day returned, to paint the Earth with gray; and my gaze moved around and didn't see her. I let out a mute cry: "Ayl! Why have you run off?" But she was in front of me and was looking for me, too; she couldn't see me and silently shouted: "Qfwfq! Where are you?" Until our eyesight darkened, examining that sooty luminosity and recognizing the outline of an eyebrow, an elbow, a thigh.

Then I wanted to shower Ayl with presents, but nothing seemed to me worthy of her. I hunted for everything that was in some way detached from the uniform surface of the world, everything marked by a speckling, a stain. But I was soon forced to realize that Ayl and I had different tastes, if not downright opposite ones: I was seeking a new world beyond the pallid patina that imprisoned everything, I examined every sign, every crack (to tell the truth something was beginning to change: in certain points the colorlessness seemed shot through with variegated flashes); instead, Ayl was a happy inhabitant of the silence that reigns where all vibration is excluded; for her anything that looked likely to break the absolute visual neutrality was a harsh discord; beauty began for her only where the grayness had extinguished even the remotest desire to be anything other than gray.

How could we understand each other? Nothing in the world that lay before our eyes was sufficient to express what we felt for each other, but while I was in a fury to wrest unknown vibrations from things, she wanted to reduce everything to the colorless beyond of their ultimate substance.

A meteorite crossed the sky, its trajectory passing in front of the Sun; its fluid and fiery envelope for an instant acted as a filter to the Sun's rays, and all of a sudden the world was immersed in a light never seen before. Purple chasms gaped at the foot of orange cliffs, and my violet hands pointed to the flaming green meteor while a thought for which words did not yet exist tried to burst from my throat:

"This for you! From me this for you, yes, yes, beautiful!"

At the same time I wheeled around, eager to see the new way Ayl would surely shine in the general transfiguration; but I didn't see her: as if in that sudden shattering of the colorless glaze, she had found a way to hide herself, to slip off among the crevices in the mosaic.

"Ayl! Don't be frightened, Ayl! Show yourself and look!"

But already the meteorite's arc had moved away from the Sun, and the Earth was reconquered by its perennial gray, now even grayer to my dazzled eyes, and indistinct, and opaque, and there was no Ayl.

She had really disappeared. I sought her through a long throbbing of days and nights. It was the era when the world was testing the forms it was later to assume: it tested them with the material it had available, even if it wasn't the most suitable, since it was understood that there was nothing definitive about the trials. Trees of smoke-colored lava stretched out twisted branches from which hung thin leaves of slate. Butterflies of ash flying over clay meadows hovered above opaque crystal daisies. Ayl might be the colorless shadow swinging from a branch of the colorless forest or bending to pick gray mushrooms under gray clumps of bushes. A hundred times I thought I glimpsed her and a hundred times I thought I lost her again. From the wastelands I moved to the inhabited localities. At that time, sensing the changes that would take place, obscure builders were shaping premature images of a remote, possible future. I crossed a piled-up metropolis of stones; I went through a mountain pierced with passageways like an anchorite's retreat; I reached a port that opened upon a sea of mud; I entered a garden where, from sandy beds, tall menhirs rose into the sky.

The gray stone of the menhirs was covered with a pattern of barely indicated gray veins. I stopped. In the center of this park, Ayl was playing with her female companions. They were tossing a quartz ball into the air and catching it.

Someone threw it too hard, the ball came within my reach, and I caught it. The others scattered to look for it; when I saw Ayl alone, I threw the ball into the air and caught it again. Ayl ran over; hiding, I threw the quartz ball, drawing Ayl farther and farther away. Finally I showed myself; she scolded me, then laughed; and so we went on, playing, through strange regions.

At that time the strata of the planet were laboriously trying to establish an equilibrium through a series of earthquakes. Every now and then the ground was shaken by one, and between Ayl and me crevasses opened across which we threw the quartz ball back and forth. These chasms gave the elements compressed in the heart of the Earth an avenue of escape, and now we saw outcroppings of rock emerge, or fluid clouds, or boiling jets spurt up.

As I went on playing with Ayl, I noticed that a gassy layer had spread over the Earth's crust, like a low fog slowly rising. A moment before it had reached our ankles, and now we were in it up to our knees, then to our hips . . . At that sight, a shadow of uncertainty and fear grew in Ayl's eyes; I didn't want to alarm her, and so, as if nothing were happening, I went on with our game; but I, too, was anxious.

It was something never seen before: an immense fluid bubble was swelling around the Earth and completely enfolding it; soon it would cover us from head to foot, and who could say what the consequences would be?

I threw the ball to Ayl beyond a crack opening in the ground, but my throw proved inexplicably shorter than I had intended and the ball fell into the gap; the ball must have become suddenly very heavy; no, it was the crack that had suddenly yawned enormously, and now Ayl was far away, beyond a liquid, wavy expanse that had opened between us and was foaming against the shore of rocks, and I leaned from this shore, shouting: "Ayl, Ayl!" and my voice, its sound, the very sound of my voice spread loudly, as I had never imagined it, and the waves rumbled still louder than my voice. In other words: it was all beyond understanding.

I put my hands to my deafened ears, and at the same moment I also felt the need to cover my nose and mouth, so as not to breathe the heady blend of oxygen and nitrogen that surrounded me, but strongest of all was the impulse to cover my eyes, which seemed ready to explode.

The liquid mass spread out at my feet had suddenly turned a new color, which blinded me, and I exploded in an articulate cry which, a little later, took on a specific meaning: "Ayl! The sea is blue!"

The great change so long awaited had finally taken place. On the Earth now there was air, and water. And over that newborn blue sea, the Sun—also colored—was setting, an absolutely different and even more violent color. So I was driven to go on with my senseless cries, like: "How red the Sun is, Ayl! Ayl! How red!"

Night fell. Even the darkness was different. I ran looking for Ayl, emitting cries without rhyme or reason, to express what I saw: "The stars are yellow, Ayl! Ayl!"

I didn't find her that night or the days and nights that followed. All around, the world poured out colors, constantly new, pink clouds gathered in violet cumuli which unleashed gilded lightning; after the storms long rainbows announced hues that still hadn't been seen, in all possible combinations. And chlorophyll was already beginning its progress: mosses and ferns grew green in the valleys where torrents ran. This was finally the setting worthy of Ayl's beauty; but she wasn't there! And without her all this varicolored sumptuousness seemed useless to me, wasted.

I ran all over the Earth, I saw again the things I had once

known gray, and I was still amazed at discovering fire was red, ice white, the sky pale blue, the earth brown, that rubies were ruby-colored, and topazes the color of topaz, and emeralds emerald. And Ayl? With all my imagination I couldn't picture how she would appear to my eyes.

I found the menhir garden, now green with trees and grasses. In murmuring pools red and blue and yellow fish were swimming. Ayl's friends were still leaping over the lawn, tossing the iridescent ball: but how changed they were! One was blonde with white skin, one brunette with olive skin, one brown-haired with pink skin, one had red hair and was dotted with countless, enchanting freckles.

"Ayl!" I cried. "Where is she? Where is Ayl? What does she look like? Why isn't she with you?"

Her friends' lips were red, their teeth white, and their tongues and gums were pink. Pink, too, were the tips of their breasts. Their eyes were aquamarine blue, cherry-black, hazel and maroon.

"Why . . . Ayl . . ." they answered. "She's gone . . . we don't know . . ." and they went back to their game.

I tried to imagine Ayl's hair and her skin, in every possible color, but I couldn't picture her; and so, as I looked for her, I explored the surface of the globe.

"If she's not up here," I thought, "that means she must be below," and at the first earthquake that came along, I flung myself into a chasm, down down into the bowels of the Earth.

"Ayl! Ayl!" I called in the darkness. "Ayl, come see how beautiful it is outside!"

Hoarse, I fell silent. And at that moment Ayl's voice, soft, calm, answered me. "Sssh. I'm here. Why are you shouting so much? What do you want?"

I couldn't see a thing. "Ayl! Come outside with me. If you only knew . . . Outside . . ."

"I don't like it, outside . . ."

"But you, before . . ."

"Before was before. Now it's different. All that confusion has come."

58

I lied. "No, no. It was just a passing change of light. Like that time with the meteorite! It's over now. Everything is the way it used to be. Come, don't be afraid . . ." If she comes out, I thought, after the first moment of bewilderment, she'll become used to the colors, she'll be happy, and she'll understand that I lied for her own good.

"Really?"

"Why should I tell you stories? Come, let me take you outside."

"No, you go ahead. I'll follow you."

"But I'm impatient to see you again."

"You'll see me only the way I like. Go ahead and don't turn around."

The telluric shocks cleared the way for us. The strata of rock opened fanwise and we advanced through the gaps. I heard Ayl's light footsteps behind me. One more quake and we were outside. I ran along steps of basalt and granite which turned like the pages of a book: already, at the end, the breach that would lead us into the open air was tearing wide, already the Earth's crust was appearing beyond the gap, sunny and green, already the light was forcing its way toward us. There: now I would see the colors brighten also on Ayl's face . . . I turned to look at her.

I heard her scream as she drew back toward the darkness, my eyes still dazzled by the earlier light could make out nothing, then the rumble of the earthquake drowned everything, and a wall of rock suddenly rose, vertically, separating us.

"Ayl! Where are you? Try to come over to this side, quickly, before the rock settles!" And I ran along the wall looking for an opening, but the smooth, gray surface was compact, without a fissure.

An enormous chain of mountains had formed at that point. As I had been projected outward, into the open, Ayl had remained beyond the rock wall, closed in the bowels of the Earth.

"Ayl! Where are you? Why aren't you out here?" and I looked around at the landscape that stretched away from my feet. Then, all of a sudden, those pea-green lawns where the first scarlet poppies were flowering, those canary-yellow fields which striped the tawny hills sloping down to a sea full of azure glints, all seemed so trivial to me, so banal, so false, so much in contrast with Ayl's person, with Ayl's world, with Ayl's idea of beauty, that I realized her place could never have been out here. And I realized, with grief and fear, that I had remained out here, that I would never again be able to escape those gilded and silvered gleams, those little clouds that turned from pale blue to pink, those green leaves that yellowed every autumn, and that Ayl's perfect world was lost forever, so lost I couldn't even imagine it any more, and nothing was left that could remind me of it, even remotely, nothing except perhaps that cold wall of gray stone.

GAMES WITHOUT END

When the galaxies become more remote, the rarefaction of the universe is compensated for by the formation of further galaxies composed of newly created matter. To maintain a stable median density of the universe it is sufficient to create a hydrogen atom every 250 million years for 40 cubic centimeters of expanding space. (This steady state theory, as it is known, has been opposed to the other hypothesis, that the universe was born at a precise moment as the result of a gigantic explosion.)

I was only a child, but I was already aware of it,—*Qfwfq narrated*,—I was acquainted with all the hydrogen atoms, one by one, and when a new atom cropped up, I noticed it right away. When I was a kid, the only playthings we had in the whole universe were the hydrogen atoms, and we played with them all the time, I and another youngster my age whose name was Pfwfp.

What sort of games? That's simple enough to explain. Since space was curved, we sent the atoms rolling along its curve, like so many marbles, and the kid whose atom went farthest won the game. When you made your shot you had to be careful, to calculate the effects, the trajectories, you had to know how to exploit the magnetic fields and the fields of gravity, otherwise the ball left the track and was eliminated from the contest.

The rules were the usual thing: with one atom you could hit another of your atoms and send it farther ahead, or else you could knock your opponent's atom out of the way. Of course, we were careful not to throw them too hard, because when two hydrogen atoms are knocked together, click! a deuterium atom might be formed, or even a helium atom, and for the purposes of the game, such atoms were out: what's more, if one of the two belonged to your opponent, you had to give him an atom of your own to pay him back.

63

You know how the curve of space is shaped: a little ball would go spinning along and then one fine moment it would start off down the slope and you couldn't catch it. So, as we went on playing, the number of atoms in the game kept getting smaller, and the first to run out of atoms was the loser.

Then, right at the crucial moment, these new atoms started cropping up. Obviously, there's quite a difference between a new atom and a used one: the new atoms were shiny, bright, fresh, and moist, as if with dew. We made new rules: one new was worth three old; and the new ones, as they were formed, were to be shared between us, fifty-fifty.

In this way our game never ended, and it never became boring either, because every time we found new atoms it seemed as if the game were new as well, as if we were playing it for the first time.

Then, what with one thing and another, as the days went by, the game grew less exciting. There were no more new atoms to be seen: the ones we lost couldn't be replaced, our shots became weak, hesitant, because we were afraid to lose the few pieces still in the game, in that barren, even space.

Pfwfp was changed, too: he became absent-minded, wandered off and couldn't be found when it was his turn to shoot; I would call him, but there was never an answer, and then he would turn up half an hour later.

"Go on, it's your turn. Aren't you in the game any more?"

"Of course I'm in the game. Don't rush me. I'm going to shoot now."

"Well, if you keep going off by yourself, we might as well stop playing!"

"Hmph! You're only making all this fuss because you're losing."

This was true: I hadn't any atoms left, whereas Pfwfp, somehow or other, always had one in reserve. If some new atoms didn't turn up for us to share, I hadn't a hope of getting even with him.

The next time Pfwfp went off, I followed him, on tiptoe. As long as I was present, he seemed to be strolling about aimlessly, whistling: but once he was out of my sight he started trotting through space, intent, like somebody who has a definite purpose in mind. And what this purpose of his was—this treachery, as you shall see—I soon discovered: Pfwfp knew all the places where new atoms were formed and every now and then he would take a little walk, to collect them on the spot the minute they were dished up, then he would hide them. This was why he was never short of atoms to play with!

But before putting them in the game, incorrigible cheat that he was, he set about disguising them as old atoms, rubbing the film of the electrons until it was worn and dull, to make me believe this was an old atom he had had all along and had just happened to find in his pocket.

And that wasn't the whole story: I made a quick calculation of the atoms played and I realized they were only a small part of those he had stolen and hid. Was he piling up a store of hydrogen? What was he going to do with it? What did he have in mind? I suddenly had a suspicion: Pfwfp wanted to build a universe of his own, a brand-new universe.

From that moment on, I couldn't rest easy: I had to get even with him. I could have followed his example: now that I knew the places, I could have gone there a little ahead of him and grabbed the new atoms the moment they were born, before he could get his hands on them! But that would have been too simple. I wanted to catch him in a trap worthy of his own perfidy. First of all, I started making fake atoms: while he was occupied with his treacherous raids, I was in a secret storeroom of mine, pounding and mixing and kneading all the material I had at my disposal. To tell you the truth, this material didn't amount to much: photoelectric radiations, scrapings from magnetic fields, a few neutrons collected in the road; but by rolling it into balls and wetting it with saliva, I managed to make it stick together. In other words, I prepared some little corpuscles that, on close inspection, were obviously not made of hydrogen or any other identifiable element, but for somebody in a hurry, like Pfwfp, who rushed past and stuck them furtively into his pocket, they looked like real hydrogen, and spanking new.

So while he still didn't suspect a thing, I preceded him in his rounds. I had made a careful mental note of all the places.

Space is curved everywhere, but in some places it's more curved than in others: like pockets or bottlenecks or niches, where the void is crumpled up. These niches are where, every two hundred and fifty million years, there is a slight tinkling sound and a shiny hydrogen atom is formed like a pearl between the valves of an oyster. I walked past, pocketed the atom, and set the fake atom in its place. Pfwfp didn't notice a thing: predatory, greedy, he filled his pockets with that rubbish, as I was accumulating all the treasures that the universe cherished in its bosom.

The fortunes of our games underwent a change: I always had new atoms to shoot, while Pfwfp's regularly missed fire. Three times he tried a roll and three times the atom crumbled to bits as if crushed in space. Now Pfwfp found one excuse after another, trying to call off the game.

"Go on," I insisted, "if you don't shoot, the game's mine."

And he said: "It doesn't count. When an atom is ruined the game's null and void, and you start over again." This was a rule he had invented at that very moment.

I didn't give him any peace, I danced around him, leaped on his back, and chanted:

> "Throw it throw it throw it
> If not, you lose, you know it.
> For every turn that you don't take
> An extra throw for me to make."

"That's enough of that," Pfwfp said, "let's change games."

"Aha!" I said. "Why don't we play at flying galaxies?"

"Galaxies?" Pfwfp suddenly brightened with pleasure. "Suits me. But you . . . you don't have a galaxy!"

"Yes, I do."

"So do I."

"Come on! Let's see who can send his highest!"

And I took all the new atoms I was hiding and flung them into space. At first they seemed to scatter, then they thickened

66

together into a kind of light cloud, and the cloud swelled and swelled, and inside it some incandescent condensations were formed, and they whirled and whirled and at a certain point became a spiral of constellations never seen before, a spiral that poised, opening in a gust, then sped away as I held on to its tail and ran after it. But now I wasn't the one who made the galaxy fly, it was the galaxy that was lifting me aloft, clinging to its tail; I mean, there wasn't any height or depth now but only space, widening, and the galaxy in its midst, also opening wide, and me hanging there, making faces at Pfwfp, who was already thousands of light-years away.

Pfwfp, at my first move, had promptly dug out all his hoard, hurling it with a balanced movement as if he expected to see the coils of an endless galaxy open in the sky. But instead, nothing happened. There was a sizzling sound of radiations, a messy flash, then everything died out at once.

"Is that the best you can do?" I shouted at Pfwfp, who was yelling curses at me, green with rage:

"I'll show you, Qfwfq, you pig!"

But in the meanwhile my galaxy and I were flying among thousands of other galaxies, and mine was the newest, the envy of the whole firmament, blazing as it was with young hydrogen and the youngest carbon and newborn beryllium. The old galaxies fled us, filled with jealousy, and we, prancing and haughty, avoided them, so antiquated and ponderous to look at. As that reciprocal flight developed, we sailed across spaces that became more and more rarefied and empty: and then I saw something appear in the midst of the void, like uncertain bursts of light. These were new galaxies, formed by matter just born, galaxies even newer than mine. Soon space became filled again, and dense, like a vineyard just before vintage time, and we flew on, escaping from one another, my galaxy fleeing the younger ones as it had the older, and young and old fleeing us. And we advanced to fly through empty skies, and these skies also became peopled, and so on and on.

In one of these propagations, I heard: "Qfwfq, you'll pay for this now, you traitor!" and I saw a brand-new galaxy flying on our trail, and there leaning forward from the very tip of the spiral, yelling threats and insults at me, was my old playmate Pfwfp.

The chase began. Where space rose, Pfwfp's galaxy, young and agile, gained ground, but on the descents, my heavier galaxy plunged ahead again.

In any kind of race there's a secret: it's all in how you take the curves. Pfwfp's galaxy tended to narrow them, mine to swing out. And as it kept broadening the curves, we were finally flung beyond the edge of space, with Pfwfp after us. We kept up the pursuit, using the system one always uses in such circumstances, that is, creating space before us as we went forward.

So there I was, with nothingness in front of me, and that nasty-faced Pfwfp after me: an unpleasant sight either way. In any case, I preferred to look ahead, and what did I see? Pfwfp, whom my eyes had just left behind me, was speeding on his galaxy directly in front of me. "Ah!" I cried, "now it's my turn to chase you!"

"What?" Pfwfp said, from before me or behind me, I'm not really sure which, "I'm the one who's chasing you!"

I turned around: there was Pfwfp, still at my heels. I looked ahead again: and he was there, racing off with his back turned to me. But as I looked more closely, I saw that in front of this galaxy of his that was preceding me there was another, and that other galaxy was mine, because there I was on it, unmistakable even though seen from behind. And I turned toward the Pfwfp following me and narrowed my eyes: I saw that his galaxy was being chased by another, mine, with me on top of it, turning at that same time to look back.

And so after every Qfwfq there was a Pfwfp, and after every Pfwfp a Qfwfq, and every Pfwfp was chasing a Qfwfq, who was pursuing him and vice versa. Our distances grew a bit shorter or a bit longer, but now it was clear that one would never overtake the other, nor the other overtake one. We had lost all pleasure in this game of chase, and we weren't children any more for that matter, but now there was nothing else we could do.

THE AQUATIC UNCLE

T*he first vertebrates who, in the*
Carboniferous period, abandoned aquatic life for terrestrial, de-
scended from the osseous, pulmonate fish whose fins were capa-
ble of rotation beneath their bodies and thus could be used as
paws on the earth.

By then it was clear that the water period was coming to an
end,—*old Qfwfq recalled,*—those who decided to make the great
move were growing more and more numerous, there wasn't a
family that didn't have some loved one up on dry land, and
everybody told fabulous tales of the things that could be done
there, and they called back to their relatives to join them.
There was no holding the young fish; they slapped their fins on
the muddy banks to see if they would work as paws, as the
more talented ones had already discovered. But just at that
time the differences among us were becoming accentuated:
there might be a family that had been living on land, say, for
several generations, whose young people acted in a way that
wasn't even amphibious but almost reptilian already; and there
were others who lingered, still living like fish, those who, in
fact, became even more fishy than they had been before.

Our family, I must say, including grandparents, was all up
on the shore, padding about as if we had never known how to
do anything else. If it hadn't been for the obstinacy of our great-
uncle N'ba N'ga, we would have long since lost all contact with
the aquatic world.

Yes, we had a great-uncle who was a fish, on my paternal
grandmother's side, to be precise, of the Coelacanthus family
of the Devonian period (the fresh-water branch: who are, for
that matter, cousins of the others—but I don't want to go into
all these questions of kinship, nobody can ever follow them
anyhow). So as I was saying, this great-uncle lived in certain

71

muddy shallows, among the roots of some protoconifers, in that inlet of the lagoon where all our ancestors had been born. He never stirred from there: at any season of the year all we had to do was push ourselves over the softer layers of vegetation until we could feel ourselves sinking into the dampness, and there below, a few palms' lengths from the edge, we could see the column of little bubbles he sent up, breathing heavily the way old folk do, or the little cloud of mud scraped up by his sharp snout, always rummaging around, more out of habit than out of the need to hunt for anything.

"Uncle N'ba N'ga! We've come to pay you a visit! Were you expecting us?" we would shout, slapping our paws and tails in the water to attract his attention. "We've brought you some insects that grow where we live! Uncle N'ba N'ga! Have you ever seen such fat cockroaches? Taste one and see if you like it . . ."

"You can clean those revolting warts you've got with your stinking cockroaches!" Our great-uncle's answer was always some remark of this sort, or perhaps even ruder: this is how he welcomed us every time, but we paid no attention because we knew he would mellow after a little while, accept our presents gladly, and converse in politer tones.

"What do you mean, Uncle? Warts? When did you ever see any warts on us?"

This business about warts was a widespread prejudice among the old fish: a notion that, from living on dry land, we would develop warts all over our bodies, exuding liquid matter: this was true enough for the toads, but we had nothing in common with them; on the contrary, our skin, smooth and slippery, was such as no fish had ever had; and our great-uncle knew this perfectly well, but he still couldn't stop larding his talk with all the slanders and intolerance he had grown up in the midst of.

We went to visit our great-uncle once a year, the whole family together. It also gave us an opportunity to have a reunion, since we were scattered all over the continent; we could exchange bits of news, trade edible insects, and discuss old questions that were still unsettled.

72

Our great-uncle spoke his mind even on questions that were removed from him by miles and miles of dry land, such as the division of territory for dragonfly hunting; and he would side with this one or that one, according to his own reasoning, which was always aquatic. "But don't you know that it's always better to hunt on the bottom and not on the water's surface? So what are you getting all upset over?"

"But, Uncle, you see: it isn't a question of hunting on the bottom or on the surface. I live at the foot of a hill, and he lives halfway up the slope . . . You know what I mean by hill, Uncle . . ."

And he said: "You always find the best crayfish at the foot of the cliffs." It just wasn't possible to make him accept a reality different from his own.

And yet, his opinions continued to exert an authority over all of us; in the end we asked his advice about matters he didn't begin to understand, though we knew he could be dead wrong. Perhaps his authority stemmed from the fact that he was a leftover from the past, from his way of using old figures of speech, like: "Lower your fins there, youngster!," whose meaning we didn't grasp very clearly.

We had made various attempts to get him up on land with us, and we went on making them; indeed, on this score, the rivalry among the various branches of the family never died out, because whoever managed to take our great-uncle home with him would achieve a position of pre-eminence over the rest of our relatives. But the rivalry was pointless, because our uncle wouldn't dream of leaving the lagoon.

"Uncle, if you only knew how sorry we feel leaving you all alone, at your age, in the midst of all that dampness . . . We've had a wonderful idea . . ." someone would begin.

"I was expecting the lot of you to catch on finally," the old fish interrupted, "now you've got over the whim of scraping around in that drought, so it's time you came back to live like normal beings. Here there's plenty of water for all, and when it comes to food, there's never been a better season for worms.

You can all dive right in, and we won't have to discuss it any further."

"No, no, Uncle N'ba N'ga, you've got it all wrong. We wanted to take you to live with us, in a lovely little meadow . . . You'll be nice and snug; we'll dig you a little damp hole. You'll be able to turn and toss in it, just like here. And you might even try taking a few steps around the place: you'll be very good at it, just wait and see. And besides, at your time of life, the climate on land is much more suitable. So come now, Uncle N'ba N'ga, don't wait to be coaxed. Won't you come home with us?"

"No!" was our great-uncle's sharp reply, and taking a nose dive into the water, he vanished from our sight.

"But why, Uncle? What have you got against the idea? We simply don't understand. Anyone as broad-minded as you ought to be above certain prejudices . . ."

From an angry huff of water at the surface, before the final plunge with a still-agile jerk of his tail fin, came our uncle's final answer: "He who has fleas in his scales swims with his belly in the mud!" which must have been an idiomatic expression (similar to our own, much more concise proverb: "If you itch, scratch"), with that term "mud" which he insisted on using where we would say "land."

That was about the time when I fell in love. Lll and I spent our days together, chasing each other; no one as quick as she had ever been seen before; in the ferns, which were as tall as trees in those days, she would climb to the top in one burst, and the tops would bend almost to the ground, then she would jump down and run off again; I, with slower and somewhat clumsier movements, followed her. We ventured into zones of the interior where no print had ever marked the dry and crusty terrain; at times I stopped, frightened at having come so far from the expanse of the lagoons. But nothing seemed so far from aquatic life as she, Lll, did: the deserts of sand and stones, the prairies, the thick forests, the rocky hillocks, the quartz mountains: this was her world, a world that seemed made especially to be scanned by her oblong eyes, to be trod by her darting steps. When you looked at her smooth skin, you felt that scales had never existed.

Her relatives made me a bit ill at ease; hers was one of those families who had become established on Earth in the earliest period and had finally become convinced they had never lived anywhere else, one of those families who, by now, even laid their eggs on dry terrain, protected by a hard shell, and Lll, if you looked at her when she jumped, at her flashing movements, you could tell she had been born the way she was now, from one of those eggs warmed by sand and sun, having completely skipped the swimming, wriggling phase of the tadpole, which was still obligatory in our less evolved families.

The time had come for Lll to meet my family: and since its oldest and most authoritative member was Great-Uncle N'ba N'ga, I couldn't avoid a visit to him, to introduce my fiancée. But every time an opportunity occurred, I postponed it, out of embarrassment; knowing the prejudices among which she had been brought up, I hadn't yet dared tell Lll that my great-uncle was a fish.

One day we had wandered off to one of those damp promontories that girdle the lagoon, where the ground is made not so much of sand as of tangled roots and rotting vegetation. And Lll came out with one of her usual dares, her challenges to feats: "Qfwfq, how long can you keep your balance? Let's see who can run closest to the edge here!" And she darted forward with her Earth-creature's leap, now slightly hesitant, however.

This time I not only felt I could follow her, but also that I could win, because my paws got a better grip on damp surfaces. "As close to the edge as you like!" I cried. "And even beyond it!"

"Don't talk nonsense!" she said. "How can you run beyond the edge? It's all water there!"

Perhaps this was the opportune moment to bring up the subject of my great-uncle. "What of that?" I said to her. "There are those who run on this side of the edge, and those who run on the other."

"You're saying things that make no sense at all!"

"I'm saying that my great-uncle N'ba N'ga lives in the water the way we live on the land, and he's never come out of it!"

"Ha! I'd like to meet this N'ba N'ga of yours!"

She had no sooner finished saying this than the muddied surface of the lagoon gurgled with bubbles, moved in a little eddy, and allowed a nose, all covered with spiky scales, to appear.

"Well, here I am. What's the trouble?" Great-Uncle said, staring at Lll with eyes as round and inexpressive as stones, flapping the gills at either side of his enormous throat. Never before had my great-uncle seemed so different from the rest of us: a real monster.

"Uncle, if you don't mind . . . this is . . . I mean, I have the pleasure to present to you my future bride, Lll," and I pointed to my fiancée, who for some unknown reason had stood erect on her hind paws, in one of her most exotic poses, certainly the least likely to be appreciated by that boorish old relative.

"And so, young lady, you've come to wet your tail a bit, eh?" my great-uncle said: a remark that in his day no doubt had been considered courtly, but to us sounded downright indecent.

I looked at Lll, convinced I would see her turn and run off with a shocked twitter. But I hadn't considered how strong her training was, her habit of ignoring all vulgarity in the world around her. "Tell me something: those little plants there . . ." she said, nonchalantly, pointing to some rushes growing tall in the midst of the lagoon, "where do they put down their roots?"

One of those questions you ask just to make conversation: as if she cared about those rushes! But it seemed Uncle had been waiting only for that moment to start explaining the why and the wherefore of the roots of floating trees and how you could swim among them and, indeed, how they were the very best places for hunting.

I thought he would never stop. I huffed impatiently, I tried to interrupt him. But what did that saucy Lll do? She encouraged him! "Oh, so you go hunting among those underwater roots? How interesting!"

I could have sunk into the ground from shame.

And he said: "I'm not fooling! The worms you find there! You can fill your belly, all right!" And without giving it a second thought, he dived. An agile dive such as I'd never seen him make before. Or rather, he made a leap into the air—his whole length out of the water, all dotted with scales—spreading the spiky fans of his fins; then, when he had completed a fine half-circle in the air, he plunged back, head-first, and disappeared quickly with a kind of screw-motion of his crescent-shaped tail.

At this sight, I recalled the little speech I had prepared hastily to apologize to Lll, taking advantage of my uncle's departure ("You really have to understand him, you know, this mania for living like a fish has finally even made him look like a fish"), but the words died in my throat. Not even I had ever realized the full extent of my grandmother's brother's fishiness. So I just said: "It's late, Lll, let's go . . ." and already my great-uncle was re-emerging, holding in his shark's lips a garland of worms and muddy seaweed.

It seemed too good to be true, when we finally took our leave; but as I trotted along silently behind Lll, I was thinking that now she would begin to make her comments, that the worst was still to come. But then Lll, without stopping, turned slightly toward me: "He's very nice, your uncle," and that was all she said. More than once in the past her irony had disarmed me; but the icy sensation that filled me at this remark was so awful that I would rather not have seen her any more than to have to face the subject again.

Instead, we went on seeing each other, going together, and the lagoon episode was never mentioned. I was still uneasy: it was no use my trying to persuade myself she had forgotten; every now and then I suspected she was remaining silent in order to embarrass me later in some spectacular way, in front of her family, or else—and, for me, this was an even worse hypothesis—she was making an effort to talk about other things only because she felt sorry for me. Then, out of a clear sky, one morning she said curtly: "See here, aren't you going to take me to visit your uncle any more?"

In a faint voice I asked: "Are you joking?"

Not at all; she was in earnest, she couldn't wait to go back and have a little chat with old N'ba N'ga. I was all mixed up.

That time our visit to the lagoon lasted longer. We lay on a sloping bank, all three of us: my great-uncle was nearest the water, but the two of us were half in and half out, too, so anyone seeing us from the distance, all close together, wouldn't have known who was terrestrial and who was aquatic.

The fish started in with one of his usual tirades: the superiority of water respiration to air breathing, and all his repertory of denigration. "Now Lll will jump up and give him what for!" I thought. Instead, that day Lll was apparently using a different tactic: she argued seriously, defending our point of view, but as if she were also taking old N'ba N'ga's notions into consideration.

According to my great-uncle, the lands that had emerged were a limited phenomenon: they were going to disappear just as they had cropped up or, in any event, they would be subject to constant changes: volcanoes, glaciations, earthquakes, upheavals, changes of climate and of vegetation. And our life in the midst of all this would have to face constant transformations, in the course of which whole races would disappear, and the only survivors would be those who were prepared to change the bases of their existence so radically that the reasons why living was beautiful would be completely overwhelmed and forgotten.

This prospect was in absolute contradiction to the optimism in which we children of the coast had been brought up, and I opposed the idea with shocked protests. But for me the true, living confutation of those arguments was Lll: in her I saw the perfect, definitive form, born from the conquest of the land that had emerged; she was the sum of the new boundless possibilities that had opened. How could my great-uncle try to deny the incarnate reality of Lll? I was aflame with polemical passion, and I thought that my fiancée was being all too patient and too understanding with our opponent.

True, even for me—used as I was to hearing only grumblings and abuse from my great-uncle's mouth—this logically arranged argumentation of his came as a novelty, though it was still spiced with antiquated and bombastic expressions and was made comical by his peculiar accent. It was also amazing to hear him display a detailed familiarity—though entirely external—with the continental lands.

But Lll, with her questions, tried to make him talk as much as possible about life under water: and, to be sure, this was the theme that elicited the most tightly knit, even emotional discourse from my great-uncle. Compared to the uncertainties of earth and air, lagoons and seas and oceans represented a future with security. Down there, changes would be very few, space and provender were unlimited, the temperature would always be steady; in short, life would be maintained as it had gone on till then, in its achieved, perfect forms, without metamorphoses or additions with dubious outcome, and every individual would be able to develop his own nature, to arrive at the essence of himself and of all things. My great-uncle spoke of the aquatic future without embellishments or illusions, he didn't conceal the problems, even serious ones, that would arise (most worrying of all, the increase of saline content); but they were problems that wouldn't upset the values and the proportions in which he believed.

"But now we gallop over valleys and mountains, Uncle!" I cried, speaking for myself but especially for Lll, who remained silent.

"Go on with you, tadpole, when you're wet again, you'll be back home!" he apostrophized, to me, resuming the tone I had always heard him use with us.

"Don't you think, Uncle, that if we wanted to learn to breathe under water, it would be too late?" Lll asked earnestly, and I didn't know whether to feel flattered because she had called my old relative uncle or confused because certain questions (at least, so I was accustomed to think) shouldn't even be asked.

"If you're game, sweetie," the fish said, "I can teach you in a minute!"

Lll came out with an odd laugh, then finally began to run away, to run on and on beyond all pursuit.

I hunted for her across plains and hills, I reached the top of a basalt spur which dominated the surrounding landscape of deserts and forests surrounded by the waters. Lll was there. What she had wanted to tell me—I had understood her!—by listening to N'ba N'ga and then by fleeing and taking refuge up here was surely this: we had to live in our world thoroughly, as the old fish lived in his.

"I'll live here, the way Uncle does down there," I shouted, stammering a bit; then I corrected myself: "The two of us will live here, together!" because it was true that without her I didn't feel secure.

But what did Lll answer me then? I blush when I remember it even now, after all these geological eras. She answered: "Get along with you, tadpole; it takes more than that!" And I didn't know whether she was imitating my great-uncle, to mock him and me at once, or whether she had really assumed the old nut's attitude toward his nephew, and either hypothesis was equally discouraging, because both meant she considered me at a halfway stage, a creature not at home in the one world or in the other.

Had I lost her? Suspecting this, I hastened to woo her back. I took to performing all sorts of feats: hunting flying insects, leaping, digging underground dens, wrestling with the strongest of our group. I was proud of myself, but unfortunately whenever I did something brave, she wasn't there to see me: she kept disappearing, and no one knew where she had gone off to hide.

Finally I understood: she went to the lagoon, where my great-uncle was teaching her to swim under water. I saw them surface together: they were moving along at the same speed, like brother and sister.

"You know?" she said, gaily, "my paws work beautifully as fins!"

"Good for you! That's a big step forward," I couldn't help remarking, sarcastically.

It was a game, for her: I understood. But a game I didn't like. I had to recall her to reality, to the future that was awaiting her.

One day I waited for her in the midst of a woods of tall ferns which sloped to the water.

"Lll, I have to talk to you," I said as soon as I saw her, "you've been amusing yourself long enough. We have more important things ahead of us. I've discovered a passage in the mountains: beyond it stretches an immense stone plain, just abandoned by the water. We'll be the first to settle there, we'll populate unknown lands, you and I, and our children."

"The sea is immense," Lll said.

"Stop repeating that old fool's nonsense. The world belongs to those with legs, not to fish, and you know it."

"I know that he's somebody who is somebody," Lll said.

"And what about me?"

"There's nobody with legs who is like him."

"And your family?"

"We've quarreled. They don't understand anything."

"Why, you're crazy! Nobody can turn back!"

"I can."

"And what do you think you'll do, all alone with an old fish?"

"Marry him. Be a fish again with him. And bring still more fish into the world. Good-by."

And with one of those rapid climbs of hers, the last, she reached the top of a fern frond, bent it toward the lagoon, and let go in a dive. She surfaced, but she wasn't alone: the sturdy, curved tail of Great-Uncle N'ba N'ga rose near hers and, together, they cleft the waters.

It was a hard blow for me. But, after all, what could I do about it? I went on my way, in the midst of the world's transformations, being transformed myself. Every now and then, among the many forms of living beings, I encountered one who "was somebody" more than I was: one who announced the future, the duck-billed platypus who nurses its young, just hatched from the egg; or I might encounter another who bore witness to a past beyond all return, a dinosaur who had sur-

vived into the beginning of the Cenozoic, or else—a crocodile—
part of the past that had discovered a way to remain immobile
through the centuries. They all had something, I know, that
made them somehow superior to me, sublime, something that
made me, compared to them, mediocre. And yet I wouldn't
have traded places with any of them.

HOW MUCH
SHALL WE BET?

The logic of cybernetics, applied to the history of the universe, is in the process of demonstrating how the galaxies, the solar system, the Earth, cellular life could not help but be born. According to cybernetics, the universe is formed by a series of feedbacks, positive and negative, at first through the force of gravity that concentrates masses of hydrogen in the primitive cloud, then through nuclear force and centrifugal force which are balanced with the first. From the moment that the process is set in motion, it can only follow the logic of this chain.

Yes, but at the beginning nobody knew it,—*Qfwfq explained,*—I mean, you could foretell it perhaps, but instinctively, by ear, guessing. I don't want to boast, but from the start I was willing to bet that there was going to be a universe, and I hit the nail on the head; on the question of its nature, too, I won plenty of bets, with old Dean $(k)yK$.

When we started betting there wasn't anything yet that might lead you to foresee anything, except for a few particles spinning around, some electrons scattered here and there at random, and protons all more or less on their own. I started feeling a bit strange, as if there was going to be a change of weather (in fact, it had grown slightly cold), and so I said: "You want to bet we're heading for atoms today?"

And Dean $(k)yK$ said: "Oh, cut it out. Atoms! Nothing of the sort, and I'll bet anything you say."

So I said: "Would you even bet ix?"

The Dean answered: "Ix raised to en!"

He had no sooner finished saying this than around each proton its electron started whirling and buzzing. An enormous hydrogen cloud was condensing in space. "You see? Full of atoms!"

"Oh, if you call *that* stuff atoms!" (k)yK said; he had the bad habit of putting up an argument, instead of admitting he had lost a bet.

We were always betting, the Dean and I, because there was really nothing else to do, and also because the only proof I existed was that I bet with him, and the only proof he existed was that he bet with me. We bet on what events would or would not take place; the choice was virtually unlimited, because up till then absolutely nothing had happened. But since there wasn't even a way to imagine how an event might be, we designated it in a kind of code: Event A, Event B, Event C, and so on, just to distinguish one from the other. What I mean is: since there were no alphabets in existence then or any other series of accepted signs, first we bet on how a series of signs might be and then we matched these possible signs with various possible events, in order to identify with sufficient precision matters that we still didn't know a thing about.

We also didn't know what we were staking because there was nothing that could serve as a stake, and so we gambled on our word, keeping an account of the bets each had won, to be added up later. All these calculations were very difficult, since numbers didn't exist then, and we didn't even have the concept of number, to begin to count, because it wasn't possible to separate anything from anything else.

This situation began to change when, in the protogalaxies, the protostars started condensing, and I quickly realized where it would all end, with that temperature rising all the time, and so I said: "Now they're going to catch fire."

"Nuts!" the Dean said.

"Want to bet?" I said.

"Anything you like," he said, and wham, the darkness was shattered by all these incandescent balls that began to swell out.

"Oh, but that isn't what catching fire means . . ." (k)yK began, quibbling about words in his usual way.

By that time I had developed a system of my own, to shut him up: "Oh, no? And what does it mean then, in your opinion?"

He kept quiet: lacking imagination as he did, when a word began to have one meaning, he couldn't conceive of its having any other.

Dean (k)yK, if you had to spend much time with him, was a fairly boring sort, without any resources, he never had anything to tell. Not that I, on the other hand, could have told much, since events worth telling about had never happened, or at least so it appeared to us. The only thing was to frame hypotheses, or rather: hypothesize on the possibility of framing hypotheses. Now, when it came to framing hypotheses of hypotheses, I had much more imagination than the Dean, and this was both an advantage and a disadvantage, because it led me to make riskier bets, so that you might say our probabilities of winning were even.

As a rule, I bet on the possibility of a certain event's taking place, whereas the Dean almost always bet against it. He had a static sense of reality, old (k)yK, if I may express myself in these terms, since between static and dynamic at that time there wasn't the difference there is nowadays, or in any case you had to be very careful in grasping it, that difference.

For example, the stars began to swell, and I said: "How much?" I tried to lead our predictions into the field of numbers, where he would have less to argue about.

At that time there were only two numbers: the number e and the number pi. The Dean did some figuring, by and large, and answered: "They'll grow to e raised to pi."

Trying to act smart! Any fool could have told that much. But matters weren't so simple, as I had realized. "You want to bet they stop, at a certain point?"

"All right. When are they going to stop?"

And with my usual bravado, I came out with my pi. He swallowed it. The Dean was dumfounded.

From that moment on we began to bet on the basis of e and of pi.

"*Pi!*" the Dean shouted, in the midst of the darkness and the scattered flashes. But instead that was the time it was e.

We did it all for fun, obviously; because there was nothing

in it for us, as far as earning went. When the elements began to be formed, we started evaluating our bets in atoms of the rarer elements, and this is where I made a mistake. I had seen that the rarest of all was technetium, so I started betting technetium and winning, and hoarding: I built up a capital of technetium. I hadn't foreseen it was an unstable element that dissolved in radiations: suddenly I had to start all over again, from zero.

Naturally, I made some wrong bets, too, but then I got ahead again and I could allow myself a few risky prognostications.

"Now a bismuth isotope is going to come out!" I said hastily, watching the newborn elements crackle forth from the crucible of a "supernova" star. "Let's bet!"

Nothing of the sort: it was a polonium atom, in mint condition.

In these cases (k)yK would snigger and chuckle as if his victories were something to be proud of, whereas he simply benefited from overbold moves on my part. Conversely, the more I went ahead, the better I understood the mechanism, and in the face of every new phenomenon, after a few rather groping bets, I could calculate my previsions rationally. The order that made one galaxy move at precisely so many million light-years from another, no more and no less, became clear to me before he caught on. After a while it was all so easy I didn't enjoy it any more.

And so, from the data I had at my disposal, I tried mentally to deduce other data, and from them still others, until I succeeded in suggesting eventualities that had no apparent connection with what we were arguing about. And I just let them fall, casually, into our conversation.

For example, we were making predictions about the curve of the galactic spirals, and all of a sudden I came out with: "Now listen a minute, (k)yK, what do you think? Will the Assyrians invade Mesopotamia?"

He laughed, confused. "Meso- what? When?"

I calculated quickly and blurted a date, not in years and centuries of course, because then the units of measuring time weren't conceivable in lengths of that sort, and to indicate a precise date we had to rely on formulas so complicated it would have taken a whole blackboard to write them down.

"How can you tell?"

"Come on, (k)yK, are they going to invade or not? I say they do; you say no. All right? Don't take so long about it."

We were still in the boundless void, striped here and there by a streak or two of hydrogen around the vortexes of the first constellations. I admit it required very complicated deductions to foresee the Mesopotamian plains black with men and horses and arrows and trumpets, but, since I had nothing else to do, I could bring it off.

Instead, in such cases, the Dean always bet no, not because he believed the Assyrians wouldn't do it, but simply because he refused to think there would ever be Assyrians and Mesopotamia and the Earth and the human race.

These bets, obviously, were long-term affairs, more than the others; not like some cases, where the result was immediately known. "You see that Sun over there, the one being formed with an ellipsoid all around it? Quick, before the planets are formed: how far will the orbits be from one another?"

The words were hardly out of my mouth when, in the space of eight or nine—what am I saying?—six or seven hundred million years, the planets started revolving each in its orbit, not a whit more narrow nor a whit wider.

I got much more satisfaction, however, from the bets we had to bear in mind for billions and billions of years, without forgetting what we had bet on, and remembering the shorter-term bets at the same time, and the number (the era of whole numbers had begun, and this complicated matters a bit) of bets each of us had won, the sum of the stakes (my advantage kept growing; the Dean was up to his ears in debt). And in addition to all this I had to dream up new bets, further and further ahead in the chain of my deductions.

"On February 8, 1926, at Santhià, in the Province of Vercelli—got that? At number 18 in Via Garibaldi—you follow me? Signorina Giuseppina Pensotti, aged twenty-two, leaves her home at quarter to six in the afternoon: does she turn right or left?"

"Mmmmm . . ." (k)yK said.

"Come on, quickly. I say she turns right . . ." And through the dust nebulae, furrowed by the orbits of the constellations, I could already see the wispy evening mist rise in the streets of Santhià, the faint light of a street lamp barely outlining the sidewalk in the snow, illuminating for a moment the slim shadow of Giuseppina Pensotti as she turned the corner past the Customs House and disappeared.

On the subject of what was to happen among the celestial bodies, I could stop making new bets and wait calmly to pocket my winnings from (k)yK as my predictions gradually came true. But my passion for gambling led me, from every possible event, to foresee the interminable series of events that followed, even down to the most marginal and aleatory ones. I began to combine predictions of the most immediately and easily calculated events with others that required extremely complicated operations. "Hurry, look at the way the planets are condensing: now tell me, which is the one where an atmosphere is going to be formed? Mercury? Venus? Earth? Mars? Come on: make up your mind! And while you're about it, calculate for me the index of demographic increase on the Indian subcontinent during the British raj. What are you puzzling over? Make it snappy!"

I had started along a narrow channel beyond which events were piling up with multiplied density; I had only to seize them by the handful and throw them in the face of my competitor, who had never guessed at their existence. Once I happened to drop, almost absently, the question: "Arsenal-Real Madrid, semifinals. Arsenal playing at home. Who wins?," and in a moment I realized that with what seemed a casual jumble of words I had hit on an infinite reserve of new combinations among the signs which compact, opaque, uniform reality would use to disguise its monotony, and I realized that perhaps the race toward the future, the race I had been the first to foresee and desire, tended only—through time and space—toward a crumbling into alternatives like this, until it would dissolve in a geometry of invisible triangles and ricochets like the course of a football among the white lines of a field as I tried to imagine them, drawn at the bottom of the luminous vortex of the planetary system, deciphering the numbers marked on the chests and backs of the players at night, unrecognizable in the distance.

By now I had plunged into this new area of possibility, gambling everything I had won before. Who could stop me? The Dean's customary bewildered incredulity only spurred me to greater risks. When I saw I was caught in a trap it was too late. I still had the satisfaction—a meager satisfaction, this time—of being the first to be aware of it: (k)yK seemed not to catch on to the fact that luck had now come over to his side, but I counted his bursts of laughter, once rare and now becoming more and more frequent . . .

"Qfwfq, have you noticed that Pharaoh Amenhotep IV had no male issue? I've won!"

"Qfwfq, look at Pompey! He lost out to Caesar after all! I told you so!"

And yet I had worked out my calculations to their conclusion, I hadn't overlooked a single component. Even if I were to go back to the beginning, I would bet the same way as before.

"Qfwfq, under the Emperor Justinian, it was the silkworm that was imported from China to Constantinople. Not gunpowder . . . Or am I getting things mixed up?"

"No, no, you win, you win . . ."

To be sure, I had let myself go, making predictions about fleeting, impalpable events, countless predictions, and now I couldn't draw back, I couldn't correct myself. Besides, correct myself how? On the basis of what?

"You see, Balzac doesn't make Lucien de Rubempré commit suicide at the end of *Les Illusions Perdues*," the Dean said, in a triumphant, squeaky little voice he had been developing of late. "He has him saved by Carlos Herrera, alias Vautrin. You know? The character who was also in *Père Goriot* . . . Now then, Qfwfq, how far have we got?"

My advantage was dropping. I had saved my winnings, converted into hard valuta, in a Swiss bank, but I had constantly to withdraw big sums to meet my losses. Not that I lost every time. I still won a bet now and then, even a big one, but the roles had been reversed; when I won I could no longer be sure it wasn't an accident or that, the next time, my calculations wouldn't again be proved wrong.

At the point we had reached, we needed reference libraries, subscriptions to specialized magazines, as well as a complex of electronic computers for our calculations: everything, as you know, was furnished us by a Research Foundation, to which, when we settled on this planet, we appealed for funds to finance our research. Naturally, our bets figure as an innocent game between the two of us and nobody suspects the huge sums involved in them. Officially we live on our modest salaries as researchers for the Electronic Predictions Center, with the added sum, for (k)yK, that goes with the position of Dean, which he intrigued to obtain from the Department, though he kept on pretending he wasn't lifting a finger. (His predilection for stasis has got steadily worse; he turned up here in the guise of a paralytic, in a wheelchair.) This title of Dean, I might add, has nothing to do with seniority, otherwise I'd be just as much entitled to it as he is, though of course it doesn't mean anything to me.

So this is how we reached our present situation. Dean (k)yK, from the porch of his building, seated in the wheelchair, his legs covered with a rug of newspapers from all over the world, which arrive with the morning post, shouts so loud you can hear him all the way across the campus: "Qfwfq, the atomic treaty between Turkey and Japan wasn't signed today; they haven't even begun talks. You see? Qfwfq, that man in Termini Imerese who killed his wife was given three years, just as I said. Not life!"

And he waves the pages of the papers, black and white the way space was when the galaxies were being formed, and crammed—as space was then—with isolated corpuscles, surrounded by emptiness, containing no destination or meaning. And I think how beautiful it was then, through that void, to draw lines and parabolas, pick out the precise point, the intersection between space and time where the event would spring forth, undeniable in the prominence of its glow; whereas now events come flowing down without interruption, like cement being poured, one column next to the other, one within the other, separated by black and incongruous headlines, legible in many ways but intrinsically illegible, a doughy mass of events without form or direction, which surrounds, submerges, crushes all reasoning.

"You know something, Qfwfq? The closing quotations on Wall Street are down 2 per cent, not 6! And that building constructed illegally on the Via Cassia is twelve stories high, not nine! Nearco IV wins at Longchamps by two lengths. What's our score now, Qfwfq?"

THE DINOSAURS

$\mathbb{T}$ *he causes of the rapid extinction of the Dinosaur remain mysterious; the species had evolved and grown throughout the Triassic and the Jurassic, and for 150 million years the Dinosaur had been the undisputed master of the continents. Perhaps the species was unable to adapt to the great changes of climate and vegetation which took place in the Cretaceous period. By its end all the Dinosaurs were dead.*

All except me,—*Qfwfq corrected,*—because, for a certain period, I was also a Dinosaur: about fifty million years, I'd say, and I don't regret it; if you were a Dinosaur in those days, you were sure you were in the right, and you made everyone look up to you.

Then the situation changed—I don't have to tell you all the details—and all sorts of trouble began, defeats, errors, doubts, treachery, pestilences. A new population was growing up on the Earth, hostile to us. They attacked us on all sides; there was no dealing with them. Now there are those who say the pleasure of decadence, the desire to be destroyed were part of the spirit of us Dinosaurs even before then. I don't know: I never felt like that; if some of the others did, it was because they sensed they were already finished.

I prefer not to think back to the period of the great death. I never believed I'd escape it. The long migration that saved me led me through a cemetery of fleshless carcasses, where only a crest or a horn or a scale of armor or a fragment of horny skin recalled the ancient splendor of the living creature. And over those remains worked the beaks, the bills, the talons, the suckers of the new masters of the planet. When at last I found no further traces, of the living or of the dead, then I stopped.

I spent many, many years on those deserted plateaus. I had survived ambushes, epidemics, starvation, frost: but I was alone.

97

To go on staying up there forever was impossible for me. I started the journey down.

The world had changed: I couldn't recognize the mountains any more, or the rivers, or the trees. The first time I glimpsed some living beings, I hid: it was a flock of the New Ones, small specimens, but strong.

"Hey, you!" They had spied me, and I was immediately amazed at this familiar way of addressing me. I ran off; they chased me. For millennia I had been used to striking terror all around me, and to feeling terror of the others' reactions to the terror I aroused. None of that now. "Hey, you!" They came over to me casually, neither hostile nor frightened.

"Why are you running? What's come over you?" They only wanted me to show them the shortest path to I don't know where. I stammered out that I was a stranger there. "What made you run off?" one of them said. "You looked as if you'd seen . . . a Dinosaur!" And the others laughed. But in that laughter I sensed for the first time a hint of apprehension. Their good humor was a bit forced. Then one of them turned serious and added: "Don't say that even as a joke. You don't know what they are . . ."

So, the terror of the Dinosaurs still continued in the New Ones, but perhaps they hadn't seen any for several generations and weren't able to recognize one. I traveled on, cautious but also impatient to repeat the experiment. At a spring a New One, a young female, was drinking; she was alone. I went up softly, stretched my neck to drink beside her; I could already imagine her desperate scream the moment she saw me, her breathless flight. She would spread the alarm, and the New Ones would come out in force to hunt me down . . . For a moment I repented my action; if I wanted to save myself, I should tear her limb from limb at once: start it all over again . . .

She turned and said: "Nice and cool, isn't it?" She went on conversing amiably, the usual remarks one makes to strangers, asking me if I came from far away, if I had run into rain on the trip, or if it had been sunny. I would never have imagined it possible to talk like that with non-Dinosaurs, and I was tense and mostly silent.

"I always come here to drink," she said, "to the Dinosaur . . ."

I reacted with a start, my eyes widening.

"Oh, yes, that's what we call it. The Dinosaur's Spring . . . that's been its name since ancient times. They say that a Dinosaur hid here, one of the last, and whenever anybody came here for a drink the Dinosaur jumped on him and tore him limb from limb. My goodness!"

I wanted to drop through the earth. "Now she'll realize who I am," I was thinking, "now she'll take a better look at me and recognize me!" And as one does, when one doesn't want to be observed, I kept my eyes lowered and coiled my tail, as if to hide it. It was such a strain that when, still smiling, she said good-by and went on her way, I felt as tired as if I'd fought a battle, one of those battles we fought when we were defending ourselves with our claws and our teeth. I realized I hadn't even said good-by back to her.

I reached the shore of a river, where the New Ones had their dens and fished for their living. To create a bend in the river, where the water would be less rapid and would hold the fish, they were constructing a dam of branches. As soon as they saw me, they glanced up from their work and stopped. They looked at me, then at each other, in silence, as if questioning one another. "This is it," I thought, "all I can do is sell my life dearly." And I prepared to leap to my defense.

Luckily, I stopped myself in time. Those fishermen had nothing against me: seeing how strong I was, they wanted to ask me if I could stay with them and work transporting wood.

"This is a safe place," they insisted, when I seemed to hesitate. "There hasn't been a Dinosaur seen here since the days of our grandfathers' grandfathers . . ."

Nobody suspected who I might be. I stayed. The climate was good, the food wasn't to my taste but it was all right, and the work wasn't too hard for one of my strength. They gave me a nickname: "The Ugly One," because I was different from them, for no other reason. These New Ones, I don't know how in the world you call them, Pantotheres or whatever, were still a rather formless species; in fact, all the other species descended from it later; and already in those days there was the greatest variety of similarities and dissimilarities from one individual to the next, so, though I was an entirely different type, I was finally convinced I didn't stand out too much.

Not that I ever became completely used to this idea: I always felt like a Dinosaur in the midst of enemies, and every evening, when they started telling stories of the Dinosaurs, legends handed down from generation to generation, I hung back in the shadow, my nerves on edge.

The stories were terrifying. The listeners, pale, occasionally bursting out with cries of fear, hung on the lips of the story-teller, whose voice also betrayed an equally profound emotion. Soon it was clear to me that all of them already knew those stories (even though the repertory was very plentiful), but when they heard them, their fear was renewed every time. The Dinosaurs were portrayed as so many monsters, described with a wealth of detail that would never have helped anyone recognize them, and depicted as intent only on harming the New Ones, as if the New Ones from the very beginning had been the Earth's most important inhabitants and we had had nothing better to do than run after them from morning till night. For myself, when I thought about us Dinosaurs, I returned in memory to a long series of hardships, death agonies, mourning; the stories that the New Ones told about us were so remote from my experience that they should have left me indifferent, as if they referred to outsiders, strangers. And yet, as I listened, I realized I had never thought about how we appeared to others, and that, among all the nonsense, those tales, here and there, from the narrators' point of view, had hit on the truth. In my mind their stories of terrors we inflicted became confused with my memories of terror undergone: the more I learned how we had made others tremble, the more I trembled myself.

Each one told a story, in turn, and at a certain point they said: "What does the Ugly One have to tell us? Don't you have any stories? Didn't anyone in your family have adventures with the Dinosaurs?"

"Yes, but . . ." I stammered, "it was so long ago . . . ah, if you only knew . . ."

The one who came to my assistance at that juncture was Fern-flower, the young creature of the spring. "Oh, leave him alone . . . He's a foreigner, he doesn't feel at home yet; he can't speak our language well enough . . ."

In the end they changed the subject. I could breathe again.

A kind of friendliness had grown up between Fern-flower and me. Nothing too intimate: I had never dared touch her. But we had long talks. Or rather, she told me all sorts of things about her life; in my fear of giving myself away, of making her suspect my identity, I stuck always to generalities. Fern-flower told me her dreams: "Last night I saw this enormous Dinosaur, terrifying, breathing smoke from his nostrils. He came closer, grabbed me by the nape, and carried me off. He wanted to eat me alive. It was a terrible dream, simply terrible, but—isn't this odd?—I wasn't the least frightened. No, I don't know how to say it . . . I liked him . . ."

That dream should have made me understand many things and especially one thing: that Fern-flower desired nothing more than to be assaulted. This was the moment for me to embrace her. But the Dinosaur they imagined was too different from the Dinosaur I was, and this thought made me even more different and timid. In other words, I missed a good opportunity. Then Fern-flower's brother returned from the season of fishing in the plains, the young one was much more closely watched, and our conversations became less frequent.

This brother, Zahn, started acting suspicious the moment he first saw me. "Who's that? Where does he come from?" he asked the others, pointing to me.

"That's the Ugly One, a foreigner, who works with the timber," they said to him. "Why? What's strange about him?"

"I'd like to ask him that," Zahn said, with a grim look. "Hey, you! What's strange about you?" What could I answer? "Me? Nothing."

"So, you're not strange, eh?" and he laughed. That time it went no further, but I was prepared for the worst.

This Zahn was one of the most active ones in the village. He had traveled about the world and seemed to know many more things than the others. When he heard the usual talk about the

Dinosaurs he was seized by a kind of impatience. "Fairy tales," he said once, "you're all telling fairy tales. I'd like to see you if a real Dinosaur turned up here."

"There haven't been any for a long time now . . ." a fisherman said.

"Not all that long . . ." Zahn sniggered. "And there might still be a herd or two around the countryside . . . In the plains, our bunch takes turns keeping watch, day and night. But there we can trust one another; we don't take in characters we don't know . . ." And he gave me a long, meaningful look.

There was no point dragging things out: better force him into the open right away. I took a step forward. "Have you got something against me?" I asked.

"I'm against anybody when we don't know who gave him birth or where he came from, and when he wants to eat our food and court our sisters . . ."

One of the fishermen took up my defense: "The Ugly One earns his keep; he's a hard worker . . ."

"He's capable of carrying tree trunks on his back, I won't deny that," Zahn went on, "but if danger came, if we had to defend ourselves with claws and teeth, how can we be sure he would behave properly?"

A general argument began. The strange thing was that the possibility of my being a Dinosaur never occurred to anyone; the sin I was accused of was being Different, a Foreigner, and therefore Untrustworthy; and the argument was over how much my presence increased the danger of the Dinosaurs' ever coming back.

"I'd like to see him in battle, with that little lizard's mouth of his . . ." Zahn went on contemptuously, goading me.

I went over to him, abruptly, nose to nose. "You can see me right now, if you don't run away."

He wasn't expecting that. He looked around. The others formed a circle. There was nothing for us to do but fight.

I moved forward, brushed off his bite by twisting my neck; I had already given him a blow of my paw that knocked him on his back, and I was on top of him. This was a wrong move;

as if I didn't know it, as if I had never seen Dinosaurs die, clawed and bitten on the chest and the belly, when they believed they had pinned down their enemy. But I still knew how to use my tail, to steady myself; I didn't want to let him turn me over; I put on pressure, but I felt I was about to give way . . .

Then one of the observers yelled: "Give it to him, Dinosaur!" No sooner had they unmasked me than I became again the Dinosaur of the old days: since all was lost, I might as well make them feel their ancient terror. And I struck Zahn once, twice, three times . . .

They tore us apart. "Zahn, we told you! The Ugly One has muscles. You don't try any tricks with him, not with old Ugly!" And they laughed and congratulated me, slapping me on the back with their paws. Convinced I had been discovered, I couldn't get my bearings; it was only later that I understood the cry "Dinosaur" was a habit of theirs, to encourage the rivals in a fight, as if to say: "Go on, you're the stronger one!" and I wasn't even sure whether they had shouted the word at me or at Zahn.

From that day on I was the most respected of all. Even Zahn encouraged me, followed me around to see me give new proofs of my strength. I must say that their usual talk about the Dinosaurs changed a bit, too, as always happens when you tire of judging things in the same old way and fashion begins to take a new turn. Now, if they wanted to criticize something in the village, they had got into the habit of saying that, among Dinosaurs, certain things were never done, that the Dinosaurs in many ways could offer an example, that the behavior of the Dinosaurs in this or that situation (in their private life, for example) was beyond reproach, and so on. In short, there seemed to be emerging a kind of posthumous admiration for these Dinosaurs about whom no one knew anything precise.

Sometimes I couldn't help saying: "Come, let's not exaggerate. What do you think a Dinosaur was, after all?"

They interrupted me: "Shut up. What do you know about them? You've never seen one."

Perhaps this was the right moment to start calling a spade a spade. "I too have seen them!" I cried, "and if you want, I can explain to you what they were like!"

They didn't believe me; they thought I was making fun of them. For me, this new way they had of talking about the Dinosaurs was almost as unbearable as the old one. Because—apart from the grief I felt at the sad fate that had befallen my species —I knew the life of the Dinosaurs from within, I knew how we had been governed by narrow-mindedness, prejudice, unable to adapt ourselves to new situations. And I now had to see them take as a model that little world of ours, so backward and so—to tell the truth—boring! I had to feel imposed on me, and by them, a kind of sacred respect for my species which I myself had never felt! But, after all, this was only right: what did these New Ones have that was so different from the Dinosaurs of the good old days? Safe in their village with their dams and their ponds, they had also taken on a smugness, a presumptuousness . . . I finally felt toward them the same intolerance I had had toward my own environment, and the more I heard them admiring the Dinosaurs the more I detested Dinosaurs and New Ones alike.

"You know something? Last night I dreamed that a Dinosaur was to go past my house," Fern-flower said to me, "a magnificent Dinosaur, a Prince or a King of Dinosaurs. I made myself pretty, I put a ribbon on my head, and I leaned out of the window. I tried to attract the Dinosaur's attention, I bowed to him, but he didn't even seem to notice me, didn't even deign to glance at me . . ."

This dream furnished me with a new key to the understanding of Fern-flower's attitude toward me: the young creature had mistaken my shyness for disdainful pride. Now, when I recall it, I realize that all I had to do was maintain that attitude a little longer, make a show of haughty detachment, and I would have won her completely. Instead, the revelation so moved me that I threw myself at her feet, tears in my eyes, and said: "No, no, Fern-flower, it's not the way you believe; you're better than any Dinosaur, a hundred times better, and I feel so inferior to you . . ."

Fern-flower stiffened, took a step backwards. "What are you

saying?" This wasn't what she expected: she was upset, and she found the scene a bit distasteful. I understood this too late; I hastily recovered myself, but a feeling of uneasiness now weighed heavily between us.

There was no time to ponder it, what with everything that happened a little later. Breathless messengers reached the village. "The Dinosaurs are coming back!" A herd of strange monsters had been sighted, speeding fiercely over the plain. At this rate they would attack the village the following morning. The alarm was sounded.

You can imagine the flood of conflicting emotions that filled my breast at this news: my species wasn't extinct, I would be able to join my brothers, take up my old life! But the memory of the old life that returned to my mind was the endless series of defeats, of flights, of dangers; to begin again meant perhaps only a temporary extension of that death agony, the return to a phase I thought had already ended. Now, here in the village, I had achieved a kind of new tranquillity, and I was sorry to lose it.

The New Ones were also torn by conflicting feelings. On the one hand, there was panic; on the other, the wish to triumph over the ancient enemy; and at the same time, there was the conviction that if the Dinosaurs had survived and were now advancing vengefully it meant nobody could stop them and their victory, pitiless as it might be, could also perhaps be a good thing for all. It was as if the New Ones wanted at the same time to defend themselves, to flee, to wipe out the enemy, and to be defeated; and this uncertainty was reflected in the disorder of their defense preparations.

"Just a moment!" Zahn shouted. "There is only one among us who is capable of taking command! The strongest of all, the Ugly One!"

"You're right! The Ugly One must command us!" the others shouted in chorus. "Yes, yes, full power to the Ugly One!" And they placed themselves at my command.

"No, no, how can I, a foreigner? . . . I'm not up to it . . ." I parried. But it was impossible to convince them.

What was I to do? That night I couldn't close my eyes. The

call of my blood insisted I should desert and join my brothers; loyalty toward the New Ones, who had welcomed and sheltered me and given me their trust, demanded I should consider myself on their side; and in addition I knew full well that neither Dinosaurs nor New Ones were worthy of my lifting a finger for them. If the Dinosaurs were trying to re-establish their rule with invasions and massacres, it meant they had learned nothing from experience, that they had survived only by mistake. And it was clear that the New Ones, turning the command over to me, had found the easiest solution: leave all responsibility to an outsider, who could be their savior but also, in case of defeat, a scapegoat to hand over to the enemy to pacify him, or else a traitor who, putting them into the enemies' hands, could bring about their unconfessable dream of being mastered by the Dinosaurs. In short, I wanted nothing to do with either side: let them rip each other apart in turn! I didn't give a damn about any of them. I had to escape as fast as possible, let them stew in their own juice, have nothing more to do with these old stories.

That same night, slipping away in the darkness, I left the village. My first impulse was to get as far as possible from the battlefield, return to my secret refuges; but curiosity got the better of me: I had to see my counterparts, to know who would win. I hid on the top of some cliffs that overhung the bend of the river, and I waited for dawn.

As the light broke, some figures appeared on the horizon. They charged forward. Even before I could distinguish them clearly, I could dismiss the notion that Dinosaurs could ever run so gracelessly. When I recognized them I didn't know whether to laugh or to blush with shame. Rhinoceroses, a herd, the first ones, big and clumsy and crude, studded with horny bumps, but basically inoffensive, devoted only to cropping grass: this is what the others had mistaken for the ancient Lords of the Earth!

The rhinoceros herd galloped with the sound of thunder, stopped to lick some bushes, then ran on toward the horizon without even noticing the waiting squads of fishermen.

I ran back to the village. "You got it all wrong! They weren't

Dinosaurs!" I announced. "Rhinoceroses, that's what they were! They've already gone. There isn't any more danger!" And I added, to justify my vanishing in the night: "I went out scouting. To spy on them and report back."

"We may not have understood they weren't Dinosaurs," Zahn said calmly, "but we have understood that you were not here," and he turned his back on me.

To be sure, they were all disappointed: about the Dinosaurs, about me. Now the stories of Dinosaurs became jokes, in which the terrible monsters played ridiculous roles. I no longer was affected by their petty wit. Now I recognized the greatness of spirit that had made us choose to disappear rather than live in a world no longer suited to us. If I survived it was only so that one of us could continue to feel himself a Dinosaur in the midst of these wretches who tried to conceal, with stupid teasing, the fear that still dominated them. And what choice did the New Ones have, beyond the choice between mockery and fear?

Fern-flower betrayed a new attitude when she narrated a dream to me: "There was this Dinosaur, very funny, all green; and everybody was teasing him and pulling his tail. Then I stepped forward and protected him; I took him away and petted him. And I realized that, ridiculous as he was, he was the saddest of all creatures and a river of tears flowed from his red and yellow eyes."

What came over me, at those words? A revulsion, a refusal to identify myself with the images of that dream, the rejection of a sentiment that seemed to have become pity, an intolerance of the diminished idea they had all conceived of the Dinosaurian dignity? I had a burst of pride; I stiffened and hurled a few contemptuous phrases in her face: "Why do you bore me with these dreams of yours? They get more childish every time! You can't dream anything but sentimental nonsense!"

Fern-flower burst into tears. I went off, shrugging my shoulders.

This happened on the dam; we weren't alone; the fishermen hadn't heard our dialogue but they had noticed my angry reaction and the young creature's tears.

Zahn felt called upon to intervene. "Who do you think you are?" he said, in a harsh voice. "How dare you insult my sister?"

I stopped, but didn't answer. If he wanted to fight, I was ready. But the mood of the village had changed in recent times: they made a joke of everything. From the group of fishermen a falsetto cry was heard: "Come off it, get along with you, Dinosaur!" This, as I well knew, was a mocking expression which had now come into use, as if to say: "Don't exaggerate, don't get carried away," and so on. But something stirred in my blood.

"Yes, I am one, if you care to know," I shouted, "a Dinosaur! That's what I am! Since you never have seen any Dinosaurs, here, take a look at me!"

General snickering broke out.

"I saw one yesterday," an old fisherman said, "he came out of the snow." Silence immediately fell all around him.

The old fellow was just back from a journey in the mountains. The thaw had melted an ancient glacier and a Dinosaur's skeleton had come to light.

The news spread through the village. "Let's go see the Dinosaur!" They all ran up the mountain, and I went with them.

When we had passed a moraine of stones, uprooted trunks, mud, and dead birds, we saw a deep, shell-shaped valley. A veil of early lichens was turning the rocks green, now that they were freed from the ice. In the midst, lying as if asleep, his neck stretched by the widened intervals of the vertebrae, his tail sown in a long serpentine, a giant Dinosaur's skeleton was lying. The chest cavity was arched like a sail, and when the wind struck the flat slabs of the ribs an invisible heart seemed to be beating within them still. The skull was turned in an anguished position, mouth open as if in a last cry.

The New Ones ran down there, shouting gaily; facing the skull, they felt the empty eye sockets staring at them; they kept a few paces' distance, silently; then they turned and resumed their silly festiveness. If one of them had looked from the skeleton to me, as I stood there staring at it, he would have realized at once that we were identical. But nobody did this. Those bones, those claws, those murderous limbs spoke a language now become illegible; they no longer said anything to anyone, except that vague name which had remained unconnected with the experiences of the present.

I continued looking at the skeleton, the Father, the Brother, my Counterpart, my Self; I recognized my fleshless limbs, my lineaments carved in the stone, everything we had been and were no longer, our majesty, our faults, our ruin.

Now these remains would be used by the planet's new, heedless occupants to mark a spot in the landscape, they would follow the destiny of the name "Dinosaur," becoming an opaque sound without meaning. I must not allow it. Everything that concerned the true nature of the Dinosaurs must remain hidden. In the night, as the New Ones slept around the skeleton, which they had decked with flags, I transported it, vertebra by vertebra, and buried my Dead.

In the morning the New Ones found not a trace of the skeleton. They didn't worry about it very long. It was another mystery added to the many mysteries concerning the Dinosaurs. They soon dismissed it from their thoughts.

But the appearance of the skeleton left its mark, for in all of them the idea of the Dinosaurs became bound to the idea of a sad end, and in the stories they now told the predominant tone was one of commiseration, of grief at our sufferings. I had no use for this pity of theirs. Pity for what? If ever a species had had a rich, full evolution, a long and happy reign, that species was ours. Our extinction had been a grandiose epilogue, worthy of our past. What could those fools understand of it? Every time I heard them become sentimental about the poor Dinosaurs I felt like making fun of them, telling invented, incredible stories. In any case, the real truth about the Dinosaurs would never be understood by anyone now; it was a secret I would keep for myself alone.

A band of vagabonds stopped at the village. Among them was a young female. When I saw her, I started with surprise. Unless my eyes were deceiving me, she didn't have only the blood of the New Ones in her veins: she was a Half-breed, a

Dinosaur Half-breed. Was she aware of it? No, certainly not, judging by her nonchalance. Perhaps it hadn't been one of her parents but one of her grandparents or great-grandparents or a more remote ancestor who had been a Dinosaur; and the features, the movements of our stock were cropping out again in her in an almost shameless fashion, now unrecognizable to the others, and to herself. She was a pretty, gay creature; she immediately had a group of suitors after her, and among them the most constant and the most smitten was Zahn.

It was early summer. The young people were giving a feast on the river. "Come with us," Zahn invited me, trying to be my friend after all our disagreements; then he immediately went back to swim at the side of the Half-breed.

I went over to Fern-flower. Perhaps the moment had come for us to speak openly, to come to an understanding. "What did you dream last night?" I asked, to break the ice.

She hung her head. "I saw a wounded Dinosaur, writhing and dying. He had bowed his noble, delicate head, and he suffered and suffered . . . I looked at him, couldn't take my eyes off him, and I realized I was feeling a strange pleasure at seeing him suffer . . ."

Fern-flower's lips were taut, evil, in an expression I had never noticed in her. I wanted only to show her that in that play of ambiguous, grim feelings I had no part: I was one who enjoyed life, I was the heir of a happy race. I started to dance around her, I splashed river water on her, waving my tail.

"You can never talk about anything that isn't sad!" I said, frivolously. "Stop it. Come and dance!"

She didn't understand me. She made a grimace.

"And if you don't dance with me, I'll dance with another!" I cried. I grasped the Half-breed by one paw, carrying her off under Zahn's nose. First he watched us move away without understanding, he was so lost in his amorous contemplation, then he was seized with jealous rage. Too late. The Half-breed and I had already dived into the river and were swimming toward the other bank, to hide in the bushes.

Perhaps I only wanted to show Fern-flower who I really was,

110

to deny the mistaken notions she had of me. And perhaps I was also moved by an old bitterness toward Zahn; I wanted to reject, ostentatiously, his new offer of friendship. Or else, more than anything, it was the familiar and yet unusual form of the Half-breed which made me desire a natural, direct relationship, without secret thoughts, without memories.

The vagabond caravan would be leaving again in the morning. The Half-breed was willing to spend the night in the bushes. I stayed there, dallying with her, until dawn.

These were only ephemeral episodes in a life otherwise calm and uneventful. I had allowed the truth about myself and the era of our domination to vanish into silence. Now they hardly ever talked about the Dinosaurs any more; perhaps nobody believed they had ever existed. Even Fern-flower had stopped dreaming of them.

When she told me: "I dreamed that in a cavern there was the sole survivor of a species whose name nobody remembered, and I went to ask it of him, and it was dark, and I knew he was there, and I couldn't see him, and I knew well who he was and what he looked like but I couldn't have expressed it, and I didn't understand if he was answering my questions or I was answering his . . ." for me this was a sign that finally an amorous understanding had begun between us, the kind I had wanted since I first stopped at the spring, when I didn't yet know if I would be allowed to survive.

Since then I had learned many things, and above all the way in which Dinosaurs conquer. First I had believed that disappearing had been, for my brothers, the magnanimous acceptance of a defeat; now I knew that the more the Dinosaurs disappear, the more they extend their dominion, and over forests far more vast than those that cover the continents: in the labyrinth of the survivors' thoughts. From the semidarkness of fears and doubts of now ignorant generations, the Dinosaurs continued to extend their necks, to raise their taloned hoofs, and when the last shadow of their image had been erased, their name went on, superimposed on all meanings, perpetuating their presence in relations among living beings. Now, when the name too had been erased, they would become one thing with the mute and anonymous molds of thought, through which thoughts take on form and substance: by the New Ones, and by those who would come after the New Ones, and those who would come even after them.

I looked around: the village that had seen me arrive as a stranger I could now rightfully call mine, and I could call Fern-flower mine, in the only way a Dinosaur could call something his. For this, with a silent wave, I said good-by to Fern-flower, left the village, and went off forever.

Along my way I looked at the trees, the rivers, and the mountains, and I could no longer distinguish the ones that had been there during the Dinosaurs' time from those that had come afterwards. Around some dens a band of vagabonds was camping. From the distance I recognized the Half-breed, still attractive, only a little fatter. To avoid being seen, I headed for the woods and observed her. She was followed by a little son, barely able to stand on his legs and wag his tail. How long had it been since I had seen a little Dinosaur, so perfect, so full of his own Dinosaur essence, and so unaware of what the word "Dinosaur" meant?

I waited for him in a clearing in the woods to watch him play, chase a butterfly, slam a pine cone against a stone to dig out the pine nuts. I went over. It was my son, all right.

He looked at me curiously. "Who are you?" he asked.

"Nobody," I said. "What about you? Do you know who you are?"

"What a question! Everybody knows that: I'm a New One!" he said.

That was exactly what I had expected to hear him say. I patted his head, said: "Good for you," and went off.

I traveled through valleys and plains. I came to a station, caught the first train, and was lost in the crowd.

THE FORM OF
SPACE

*T*he equations of the gravitational field which relate the curve of space to the distribution of matter are already becoming common knowledge.

To fall in the void as I fell: none of you knows what that means. For you, to fall means to plunge perhaps from the twenty-sixth floor of a skyscraper, or from an airplane which breaks down in flight: to fall headlong, grope in the air a moment, and then the Earth is immediately there, and you get a big bump. But I'm talking about the time when there wasn't any Earth underneath or anything else solid, not even a celestial body in the distance capable of attracting you into its orbit. You simply fell, indefinitely, for an indefinite length of time. I went down into the void, to the most absolute bottom conceivable, and once there I saw that the extreme limit must have been much, much farther below, very remote, and I went on falling, to reach it. Since there were no reference points, I had no idea whether my fall was fast or slow. Now that I think about it, there weren't even any proofs that I was really falling: perhaps I had always remained immobile in the same place, or I was moving in an upward direction; since there was no above or below these were only nominal questions and so I might just as well go on thinking I was falling, as I was naturally led to think.

Assuming then that one was falling, everyone fell with the same speed and rate of acceleration; in fact we were always more or less on the same level: I, Ursula H'x, Lieutenant Fenimore. I didn't take my eyes off Ursula H'x: she was very beautiful to see, and in falling she had an easy, relaxed attitude. I hoped I would be able sometimes to catch her eye, but as she fell, Ursula H'x was always intent on filing and polishing her nails or running her comb through her long, smooth hair, and she never glanced toward me. Nor toward Lieutenant Fenimore,

I must say, though he did everything he could to attract her attention.

Once I caught him—he thought I couldn't see him—as he was making some signals to Ursula H'x: first he struck his two index fingers, outstretched, one against the other, then he made a rotating gesture with one hand, then he pointed down. I mean, he seemed to hint at an understanding with her, an appointment for later on, in some place down there, where they were to meet. All nonsense, I knew perfectly well: there were no meetings possible among us, because our falls were parallel and the same distance always remained between us. But the mere fact that Lieutenant Fenimore had got such ideas into his head—and tried to put them into the head of Ursula H'x—was enough to get on my nerves, even though she paid no attention to him, indeed she made a slight blurting sound with her lips, directed—I felt there was no doubt—at him. (Ursula H'x fell, revolving with lazy movements as if she were turning in her bed and it was hard to say whether her gestures were directed at someone else or whether she was playing for her own benefit, as was her habit.)

I too, naturally, dreamed only of meeting Ursula H'x, but since, in my fall, I was following a straight line absolutely parallel to the one she followed, it seemed inappropriate to reveal such an unattainable desire. Of course, if I chose to be an optimist, there was always the possibility that, if our two parallels continued to infinity, the moment would come when they would touch. This eventuality gave me some hope; indeed, it kept me in a state of constant excitement. I don't mind telling you I had dreamed so much of a meeting of our parallels, in great detail, that it was now a part of my experience, as if I had actually lived it. Everything would happen suddenly, with simplicity and naturalness: after the long separate journey, unable to move an inch closer to each other, after having felt her as an alien being for so long, a prisoner of her parallel route, then the consistency of space, instead of being impalpable as it had always been, would become more taut and, at the same time, looser, a condensing of the void which would seem to come not from outside but from within us, and would press me and Ursula H'x together (I had only to shut my eyes to see her come forward, in an attitude I recognized as hers even if it was different from all her habitual attitudes: her arms stretched down, along her sides, twisting her wrists as if she were stretching and at the same time writhing and leaning forward), and then the invisible line I was following would become a single line, occupied by a mingling of her and me where her soft and secret nature would be penetrated or rather would enfold and, I would say, almost absorb the part of myself that till then had been suffering at being alone and separate and barren.

Even the most beautiful dreams can suddenly turn into nightmares, and it then occurred to me that the meeting point of our two parallels might also be the point at which all parallels existing in space eventually meet, and so it would mark not only my meeting with Ursula H'x but also—dreadful prospect—a meeting with Lieutenant Fenimore. At the very moment when Ursula H'x would cease to be alien to me, another alien with his thin black mustache would share our intimacies in an inextricable way: this thought was enough to plunge me into the most tormented jealous hallucinations: I heard the cry that our meeting —hers and mine—tore from us melt in a spasmodically joyous unison and then—I was aghast at the presentiment—from that sound burst her piercing cry as she was violated—so, in my resentful bias, I imagined—from behind, and at the same time the Lieutenant's vulgar shout of triumph, but perhaps—and here my jealousy became delirium—these cries of theirs, hers and his—might also not be so different or so dissonant, they might also achieve a unison, be joined in a single cry of downright pleasure, distinct from the sobbing, desperate moan that would burst from my lips.

In this alternation of hopes and apprehensions I continued to fall, constantly peering into the depths of space to see if anything heralded an immediate or future change in our condition. A couple of times I managed to glimpse a universe, but it was far away and seemed very tiny, well off to the right or to the left; I barely had time to make out a certain number of galaxies like shining little dots collected into superimposed masses which revolved with a faint buzz, when everything would vanish as it had appeared, upwards or to one side, so that I began to suspect it had only been a momentary glare in my eyes.

"There! Look! There's a universe! Look over there! There's something!" I shouted to Ursula H'x, motioning in that direction; but, tongue between her teeth, she was busy caressing the smooth, taut skin of her legs, looking for those very rare and almost invisible excess hairs she could uproot with a sharp tug of her pincerlike nails, and the only sign she had heard my call might be the way she stretched one leg upwards, as if to exploit —you would have said—for her methodical inspection the dim light reflected from that distant firmament.

I don't have to tell you the contempt Lieutenant Fenimore displayed toward what I might have discovered on those occasions: he gave a shrug—shaking his epaulettes, his bandoleer, and the decorations with which he was pointlessly arrayed—and turned in the other direction, snickering. Unless he was the one (when he was sure I was looking elsewhere) who tried to arouse Ursula's curiosity (and then it was my turn to laugh, seeing that her only response was to revolve in a kind of somersault, turning her behind to him: a gesture no doubt disrespectful but lovely to see, so that, after rejoicing in my rival's humiliation, I caught myself envying him this, as a privilege), indicating a labile point fleeing through space, shouting: "There! There! A universe! This big! I saw it! It's a universe!"

I won't say he was lying: statements of that sort, as far as I know, were as likely to be true as false. It was a proved fact that, every now and then, we skirted a universe (or else a universe skirted us), but it wasn't clear whether these were a number of universes scattered through space or whether it was always the same universe we kept passing, revolving in a mysterious trajectory, or whether there was no universe at all and what we thought we saw was the mirage of a universe which perhaps had once existed and whose image continued to rebound from the walls of space like the rebounding of an echo. But it could also be that the universes had always been there,

118

dense around us, and had no idea of moving, and we weren't moving, either, and everything was arrested forever, without time, in a darkness punctuated only by rapid flashes when something or someone managed for a moment to free himself from that sluggish timelessness and indicate the semblance of a movement.

All these hypotheses were equally worth considering, but they interested me only insofar as they concerned our fall and the possibility of touching Ursula H'x. In other words, nobody really knew anything. So why did that pompous Fenimore sometimes assume a superior manner, as if he were certain of things? He had realized that when he wanted to infuriate me the surest system was to pretend to a long-standing familiarity with Ursula H'x. At a certain point Ursula took to swaying as she came down, her knees together, shifting the weight of her body this way and that, as if wavering in an ever-broader zigzag: just to break the monotony of that endless fall. And the Lieutenant then also started swaying, trying to pick up her rhythm, as if he were following the same invisible track, or rather as if he were dancing to the sound of the same music, audible only to the two of them, which he even pretended to whistle, putting into it, on his own, a kind of unspoken understanding, as if alluding to a private joke among old boozing companions. It was all a bluff—I knew that, of course—but still it gave me the idea that a meeting between Ursula H'x and Lieutenant Fenimore might already have taken place, who knows how long ago, at the beginning of their trajectories, and this suspicion gnawed at me painfully, as if I had been the victim of an injustice. On reflecting, however, I reasoned that if Ursula and the Lieutenant had once occupied the same point in space, this meant that their respective lines of fall had since been moving apart and presumably were still moving apart. Now, in this slow but constant removal from the Lieutenant, it was more than likely that Ursula was coming closer to me; so the Lieutenant had little to boast of in his past conjunctions: I was the one at whom the future smiled.

The process of reasoning that led me to this conclusion was

not enough to reassure me at heart: the possibility that Ursula H'x had already met the Lieutenant was in itself a wrong which, if it had been done to me, could no longer be redeemed. I must add that past and future were vague terms for me, and I couldn't make much distinction between them: my memory didn't extend beyond the interminable present of our parallel fall, and what might have been before, since it couldn't be remembered, belonged to the same imaginary world as the future, and was confounded with the future. So I could also suppose that if two parallels had ever set out from the same point, these were the lines that Ursula H'x and I were following (in this case it was nostalgia for a lost oneness that fed my eager desire to meet her); however, I was reluctant to believe in this hypothesis, because it might imply a progressive separation and perhaps her future arrival in the braid-festooned arms of Lieutenant Fenimore, but chiefly because I couldn't get out of the present except to imagine a different present, and none of the rest counted.

Perhaps this was the secret: to identify oneself so completely with one's own state of fall that one could realize the line followed in falling wasn't what it seemed but another, or rather to succeed in changing that line in the only way it could be changed, namely, by making it become what it had really always been. It wasn't through concentrating on myself that this idea came to me, though, but through observing, with my loving eye, how beautiful Ursula H'x was even when seen from behind, and noting, as we passed in sight of a very distant system of constellations, an arching of her back and a kind of twitch of her behind, but not so much the behind itself as an external sliding that seemed to rub past the behind and cause a not unpleasant reaction from the behind itself. This fleeting impression was enough to make me see our situation in a new way: if it was true that space with something inside is different from empty space because the matter causes a curving or a tautness which makes all the lines contained in space curve or tauten, then the line each of us was following was straight in the only way a straight line can be straight: namely, deformed to the extent that the limpid harmony of the general void is deformed by the clutter of matter, in other words, twisting all around this bump or pimple or excrescence which is the universe in the midst of space.

My point of reference was always Ursula and, in fact, a certain way she had of proceeding as if twisting could make more familiar the idea that our fall was like a winding and unwinding in a sort of spiral that tightened and then loosened. However, Ursula—if you watched her carefully—wound first in one direction, then in the other, so the pattern we were tracing was more complicated. The universe, therefore, had to be considered not a crude swelling placed there like a turnip, but as an angular, pointed figure where every dent or bulge or facet corresponded to other cavities and projections and notchings of space and of the lines we followed. This, however, was still a schematic image, as if we were dealing with a smooth-walled solid, a compenetration of polyhedrons, a cluster of crystals; in reality the space in which we moved was all battlemented and perforated, with spires and pinnacles which spread out on every side, with cupolas and balustrades and peristyles, with rose windows, with double- and triple-arched fenestrations, and while we felt we were plunging straight down, in reality we were racing along the edge of moldings and invisible friezes, like ants who, crossing a city, follow itineraries traced not on the street cobbles but along walls and ceilings and cornices and chandeliers. Now if I say city it amounts to suggesting figures that are, in some way, regular, with right angles and symmetrical proportions, whereas instead, we should always bear in mind how space breaks up around every cherry tree and every leaf of every bough that moves in the wind, and at every indentation of the edge of every leaf, and also it forms along every vein of the leaf, and on the network of veins inside the leaf, and on the piercings made every moment by the riddling arrows of light, all printed in negative in the dough of the void, so that there is nothing now that does not leave its print, every possible print of every possible thing, and together every transformation of these prints, instant by instant, so the pimple growing on a caliph's nose or the soap bubble resting on a laundress's bosom changes the general form of space in all its dimensions.

All I had to do was understand that space was made in this

way and I realized there were certain soft cavities hollowed in it as welcoming as hammocks where I could lie joined with Ursula H'x, the two of us swaying together, biting each other in turn along all our persons. The properties of space, in fact, were such that one parallel went one way, and another in another way: I for example was plunging within a tortuous cavern while Ursula H'x was being sucked along a passage communicating with that same cavern so that we found ourselves rolling together on a lawn of algae in a kind of subspatial island, writhing, she and I, in every pose, upright and capsized, until all of a sudden our two straight lines resumed their distance, the same as always, and each continued on its own as if nothing had happened.

The grain of space was porous and broken with crevasses and dunes. If I looked carefully, I could observe when Lieutenant Fenimore's course passed through the bed of a narrow, winding canyon; then I placed myself on the top of a cliff and, at just the right moment, I hurled myself down on him, careful to strike him on the cervical vertebrae with my full weight. The bottom of such precipices in the void was stony as the bed of a dried-up stream, and Lieutenant Fenimore, sinking to the ground, remained with his head stuck between two spurs of rock; I pressed one knee into his stomach, but he meanwhile was crushing my knuckles against a cactus's thorns—or the back of a porcupine? (spikes, in any case, of the kind corresponding to certain sharp contractions of space)—to prevent me from grabbing the pistol I had kicked from his hand. I don't know how I happened, a moment later, to find myself with my head thrust into the stifling granulosity of the strata where space gives way, crumbling like sand; I spat, blinded and dazed; Fenimore had managed to collect his pistol; a bullet whistled past my ear, ricocheting off a proliferation of the void that rose in the shape of an anthill. And I fell upon him, my hands at his throat, to strangle him, but my hands slammed against each other with a "plop!": our paths had become parallel again, and Lieutenant Fenimore and I were descending, maintaining our customary distance, ostentatiously turning our backs on each other, like two people

122

who pretend they have never met, haven't even seen each other before.

What you might consider straight, one-dimensional lines were similar, in effect, to lines of handwriting made on a white page by a pen that shifts words and fragments of sentences from one line to another, with insertions and cross-references, in the haste to finish an exposition which has gone through successive, approximate drafts, always unsatisfactory; and so we pursued each other, Lieutenant Fenimore and I, hiding behind the loops of the *l*'s, especially the *l*'s of the word "parallel," in order to shoot and take cover from the bullets and pretend to be dead and wait, say, till Fenimore went past in order to trip him up and drag him by his feet, slamming his chin against the bottoms of the *v*'s and the *u*'s and the *m*'s and the *n*'s which, written all evenly in an italic hand, became a bumpy succession of holes in the pavement (for example, in the expression "unmeasurable universe"), leaving him stretched out in a place all trampled with erasings and x-ings, then standing up there again, stained with clotted ink, to run toward Ursula H'x, who was trying to act sly, slipping behind the tails of the *f* which trail off until they become wisps, but I could seize her by the hair and bend her against a *d* or a *t* just as I write them now, in haste, bent, so you can recline against them, then we might dig a niche for ourselves down in a *g*, in the *g* of "big," a subterranean den which can be adapted as we choose to our dimensions, being made more cozy and almost invisible or else arranged more horizontally so you can stretch out in it. Whereas naturally the same lines, rather than remain series of letters and words, can easily be drawn out in their black thread and unwound in continuous, parallel, straight lines which mean nothing beyond themselves in their constant flow, never meeting, just as we never meet in our constant fall: I, Ursula H'x, Lieutenant Fenimore, and all the others.

THE LIGHT-YEARS

The more distant a galaxy is, the more swiftly it moves away from us. A galaxy located at ten billion light-years from us would have a speed of recession equal to the speed of light, three hundred thousand kilometers per second. The "quasi-stars" recently discovered are already approaching this threshold.

One night I was, as usual, observing the sky with my telescope. I noticed that a sign was hanging from a galaxy a hundred million light-years away. On it was written: I SAW YOU. I made a quick calculation: the galaxy's light had taken a hundred million years to reach me, and since they saw up there what was taking place here a hundred million years later, the moment when they had seen me must date back two hundred million years.

Even before I checked my diary to see what I had been doing that day, I was seized by a ghastly presentiment: exactly two hundred million years before, not a day more nor a day less, something had happened to me that I had always tried to hide. I had hoped that with the passage of time the episode had been completely forgotten; it was in sharp contrast—at least, so it seemed to me—with my customary behavior before and after that date: so, if ever anybody wanted to dig up that business again, I was ready to deny it quite calmly, and not only because it would have been impossible to furnish proof, but also because an action determined by such exceptional conditions—even if it was really verified—was so improbable that it could be considered untrue in all good faith, even by me. Instead, from a distant celestial body, here was somebody who had seen me, and the story was cropping up again, now of all times.

Naturally, I was in a position to explain everything that had happened, and what caused it to happen, and to make my own behavior completely comprehensible, if not excusable. I thought

127

of replying at once with a sign, using a phrase in my own defense, like LET ME EXPLAIN or else I'D LIKE TO HAVE SEEN YOU IN MY PLACE, but this wouldn't have been enough and the things that would have to be said were too many to be compressed into a short statement legible at such a distance. And above all, I had to be careful not to make a misstep, not to reinforce with an explicit admission what that I SAW YOU merely hinted at. In short, before leaving myself open with any declaration I would have to know exactly what they had seen from the galaxy and what they hadn't: and for this purpose all I could do was ask, using a sign on the order of DID YOU REALLY SEE EVERYTHING OR JUST A LITTLE BIT? or perhaps LET'S SEE IF YOU'RE TELLING THE TRUTH: WHAT WAS I DOING?, then I would have to wait long enough for them to be able to see my sign, and then an equally long period until I could see their answer and attend to the necessary rectifications. All this would take another two hundred million years, or rather a few million years more, because while the images were coming and going with the speed of light, the galaxies continued to move apart, therefore that constellation now was no longer where I had seen it, but a bit farther on, and the image of my sign would have to chase it. I mean, it was a slow system, which would have obliged me to discuss again, more than four hundred million years after they had happened, those events that I wanted to make everyone forget in the shortest possible time.

I thought the best line to take was to act as if nothing had happened, minimize the importance of what they might have found out. So I hastened to expose, in full view, a sign on which I had written simply: WHAT OF IT? If up in the galaxy they had thought they would embarrass me with their I SAW YOU, my calm would disconcert them, and they would be convinced there was no point in dwelling on that episode. If, at the same time, they didn't have much information against me, a vague expression like WHAT OF IT? would be useful as a feeler, to see how seriously I should take their affirmation I SAW YOU. The distance separating us (from its dock of a hundred million light-years the galaxy had sailed a million centuries before, journeying into the darkness) would perhaps make it less obvious that my WHAT OF IT? was replying to their I SAW YOU of two hundred million years before, but it didn't seem wise to include more explicit references in the new sign, because if the memory of that day, after three million centuries, was becoming dim, I certainly didn't want to be the one to refresh it.

After all, the opinion they might have formed of me, on that single occasion, shouldn't worry me too much. The facts of my life, the ones that had followed, after that day, for years and centuries and millennia, testified—at least the great majority of them—in my favor; so I had only to let the facts speak for themselves. If, from that distant celestial body, they had seen what I was doing one day two hundred million years ago, they must have seen me also the following day, and the day after that, and the next and the next, and they would gradually have modified the first negative opinion of me they might have formed, hastily, on the basis of an isolated episode. In fact, when I thought how many years had already gone by since that I SAW YOU, I was convinced the bad impression must now have been erased by time and followed by a probably positive evaluation, or one, in any case, that corresponded more to reality. However, this rational certainty was not enough to afford me relief: until I had the proof of a change of opinion in my favor, I would remain uneasy at having been caught in an embarrassing position and identified with it, nailed fast in that situation.

Now you will say I could very well have shrugged off the opinion of me held by some strangers living on a remote constellation. As a matter of fact, what worried me wasn't the limited opinion of this or that celestial body, but the suspicion that the consequences of their having seen might be limitless. Around that galaxy there were many others, some with a radius shorter by a hundred million light-years, with observers who kept their eyes open: the I SAW YOU sign, before I had glimpsed it, had certainly been read by inhabitants of other celestial bodies, and the same thing would have happened afterwards on the gradually more distant constellations. Even if no one could know precisely to what specific situation that I SAW YOU referred, this indefiniteness would not in the least be to my advantage. On the contrary, since people are always ready to believe the worst, what I might really have been seen doing at a distance of a hundred million light-years was, after all, nothing compared to everything that elsewhere they might imagine had been seen. The bad impression I may have left during that moment of heedlessness two million centuries ago would then be enlarged and multiplied, refracted across all the galaxies of the universe, nor was it possible for me to deny it without making the situation worse, since, not knowing what extreme and slanderous deductions those who hadn't directly seen me might have come to, I had no idea where to begin and where to end my denials.

In this state of mind, I kept looking around every night with my telescope. And after two nights I noticed that on a galaxy at a distance of a hundred million years and one light-day they had also put up a sign I SAW YOU. There could be no doubt that they were also referring to that time: what I had always tried to hide had been discovered not by only one celestial body but also by another located in quite a different zone in space. And by still others: in the nights that followed I continued to see new signs with I SAW YOU on them, set on different constellations every time. From a calculation of the light-years it emerged that the moment when they had seen me was always the same. To each of these I SAW YOUs I answered with signs marked by contemptuous indifference, such as OH REALLY? HOW NICE or else FAT LOT I CARE, or else by an almost provocative mockery, such as TANT PIS or else LOOK! IT'S ME!, but still retaining my reserve.

Though the logic of the situation led me to regard the future with reasonable optimism, the convergence of all those I SAW YOUs on a single point in my life, a convergence surely fortuitous, due to special conditions of interstellar visibility (the single exception was one celestial body where, corresponding to that same date, a sign appeared saying WE CAN'T SEE A DAMN THING), kept me in a constant state of nerves.

It was as if in the space containing all the galaxies the image of what I had done that day were being projected in the interior of a sphere that swelled constantly, at the speed of light: the observers of the celestial bodies that gradually came within the sphere's radius were enabled to see what had happened. Each of these observers could, in turn, be considered the center of a sphere also expanding at the speed of light, projecting the words I SAW YOU on their signs all around. At the same time, all these celestial bodies belonged to galaxies moving away from one another in space at a speed proportional to the distance, and every observer who indicated he had received a message, before he could receive a second one, had already moved off through space at a constantly increasing speed. At a certain point the farthest galaxies that had seen me (or had seen the I SAW YOU sign from a galaxy closer to us, or the I SAW THE I SAW YOU from a bit farther on) would reach the ten-billion-light-year threshold, beyond which they would move off at three hundred thousand kilometers per second, the speed of light, and no image would be able to overtake them after that. So there was the risk that they would remain with their temporary mistaken opinion of me, which from that moment on would become definitive, no longer rectifiable, beyond all appeal and therefore, in a sense, correct, corresponding to the truth.

So it was indispensable to clear up the misunderstanding as quickly as possible. And to clear it up, I could hope for only one thing: that, after that occasion, I had been seen other times, when I gave another image of myself, the one that was—I had no doubts on this score—the true image of me that should be remembered. In the course of the last two hundred million years, there had been no lack of opportunities, and for me just one, very clear, would be enough, to avoid confusion. Now, for example, I recalled a day when I had really been myself, I mean myself in the way I wanted others to see me. This day—I calculated rapidly—had been exactly one hundred million years ago. So, on the galaxy a hundred million light-years away they were seeing me at this very moment in that situation so flattering to my prestige, and their opinion of me was surely changing, modifying, or rather refuting that first fleeting impression. Right now, or thereabouts: because now the distance that separated us was no longer a hundred million light-years, but a hundred and one; anyhow I had only to wait an equal number of years to allow the light there to arrive here (the date when that would happen was easily calculated, bearing Hubble's constant in mind) and then I would learn their reaction.

Those who had managed to see me at moment x would, all the more surely, have seen me at moment y, and since my image in y was much more convincing than in x—indeed, I would call it more inspiring, unforgettable—they would remember me in y, whereas what had been seen of me in x would be forgotten immediately, erased, perhaps after having been fleetingly recalled to mind, in a kind of dismissal, as if to say: Just think, one who is like y can by chance be seen as x and you might believe he *is* x although it's clear that he's absolutely y.

I was almost cheered by the number of I SAW YOUS still appearing all around, because it meant that interest in me was aroused and therefore my more radiant day would escape no one. It would have had (or rather, was already having, beyond my knowledge) a much wider resonance than the sort—limited to given surroundings and, moreover, I must admit, rather marginal—which I, in my modesty, had formerly expected.

You must also consider those celestial bodies from which—through absent-mindedness or bad placing—they hadn't seen me but only a nearby I SAW YOU sign; they had also set up signs saying: LOOKS AS IF THEY'VE SEEN YOU or else FROM WHERE THEY ARE THEY CAN SEE YOU! (expressions in which I sensed a touch of curiosity or of sarcasm); on those bodies, too, there were eyes trained on me and now, precisely because they had missed one opportunity, they would hardly allow a second to escape them, and having received only indirect and hearsay information about x, they would be all the more ready to accept y as the only true reality concerning me.

So the echo of the moment y would be propagated through time and space, it would reach the most distant, the fastest galaxies, and they would elude all further images, racing at light's speed of three hundred thousand kilometers per second and taking that now definitive image of me beyond time and space, where it would become the truth containing in its sphere with unlimited radius all the other spheres with their partial and contradictory truths.

A hundred million centuries or so, after all, aren't an eternity, but to me they seemed never to go by. Finally the night arrived: I had long since aimed my telescope at that same galaxy of the first time. I moved my right eye, its lid half closed, to the eyepiece, I raised my eyelid slowly, and there was the constellation, perfectly framed, and there was a sign in its midst, the words as yet indistinct. I focused better . . . There was written: TRA-LA-LA-LA. Just that: TRA-LA-LA-LA. At the moment when I had expressed the essence of my personality, with abundant evidence and with no risk of misinterpretation, at the moment when I had furnished the key to interpreting all the acts of my past and future life and to forming an over-all and objective opinion, what had they seen, they who had not only the opportunity but also the moral obligation to observe and note what I was doing? They hadn't seen anything, hadn't been aware of anything, hadn't observed anything special. To discover that such a great part of my reputation was at the mercy of a character who was so untrustworthy left me prostrate. That proof of myself, which—because of the various favorable circumstances that had accompanied it—I considered incapable of repetition, had gone by unobserved, wasted, definitely lost for a whole zone of the universe, only because that gentleman had allowed himself five minutes of idleness, of relaxation, we might as well say of irresponsibility, his head in the air like an idiot, perhaps in the euphoria of someone who has had a drop too much, and on his sign he had found nothing better to write than a meaningless scrawl, perhaps the silly tune that he had been whistling, forgetting his duties, TRA-LA-LA-LA.

Only one thought afforded me some comfort: the thought that on the other galaxies there were bound to be more diligent observers. Until then I had never been so pleased at the great number of spectators that the old, and unfortunate, episode had had; now they would be ready to perceive the new situation. I returned to the telescope, night after night. A few nights later

133

a galaxy at the proper distance appeared to me in all its splendor. It had a sign. And on it was written this sentence: YOU HAVE A FLANNEL UNDERSHIRT.

Tears in my eyes, I racked my brain for an explanation. Perhaps in that place, with the passage of time, they had so perfected their telescopes that they amused themselves by observing the most insignificant details, the undershirt a person wore, whether it was flannel or cotton, and all the rest meant nothing to them, they paid no attention to it at all. And, for them, my honorable act, my—shall we say?—magnanimous and generous act, had gone for nothing; they had retained only one element, my flannel undershirt: an excellent undershirt, to be sure, and perhaps at another moment I would have been pleased at their noticing it, but not then, oh no, not then.

In any case, I had many other witnesses awaiting me: it was only natural that, out of the whole number, some should fail; I wasn't the sort of person to become distraught over such a little setback. In fact, from a galaxy a bit farther on, I finally had the proof that someone had seen perfectly how I had behaved and had evaluated my action properly, that is, enthusiastically. Indeed, on a sign he had written: THAT CHARACTER'S REALLY ON THE BALL. I noted it with complete satisfaction— a satisfaction, mind you, which merely confirmed my expectation, or rather my certainty that my merits would be suitably recognized—but then the expression THAT CHARACTER attracted my attention. Why did they call me THAT CHARACTER, if they already knew me and had seen me, even in that unfortunate circumstance? Shouldn't I be quite familiar to them already? With some adjustment, I improved the focus of my telescope and discovered, at the bottom of the same sign, another sentence written in smaller letters: WHO THE HELL CAN HE BE? Can you imagine a worse stroke of luck? Those who held the key to understanding who I really was hadn't recognized me. They hadn't connected this praiseworthy episode with that deplorable incident two hundred million years earlier, so the deplorable incident was still attributed to me, and the other wasn't, the other remained an impersonal, anonymous anecdote, which didn't belong to anyone's history.

My first impulse was to brandish a sign: IT'S ME! I gave up the idea: what would be the good of it? They would see it more than a hundred million years after moment x had gone by; we were approaching the half-billion mark; to be sure of making myself understood I would have to specify, dig up that old business again, and this was just what I wanted most to avoid.

By now I had lost my self-confidence. I was afraid I wouldn't receive any greater amends from the other galaxies, either. Those who had seen me had seen me in a partial, fragmentary, careless way, or had understood only up to a point what was happening, missing the essential quality, not analyzing the elements of my personality which, from one situation to the next, were thrown into relief.

Only one sign said what I had really been expecting: YOU KNOW SOMETHING? YOU'RE REALLY ON THE BALL! I hastened to leaf through my notebook, to see what reactions had come from that galaxy at moment x. By coincidence, that was the very place where the sign had appeared saying WE CAN'T SEE A DAMN THING. In that zone of the universe, I surely enjoyed a higher esteem, no denying that, and I ought to have rejoiced at last, but instead I felt no satisfaction at all. I realized that, since these admirers of mine weren't those who might earlier have formed an unfavorable opinion of me, I didn't give a damn about them. The assurance that moment y had refuted and erased moment x couldn't come to me from them, and my uneasiness continued, exacerbated by the great length of time and by my not knowing whether the causes of my dismay were there and whether or not they would be dispelled.

Naturally, for the observers scattered over the universe, moment x and moment y were only two among countless observable moments, and in fact, every night on the constellations located at the most varied distances signs appeared referring to other episodes, signs saying STRAIGHT AHEAD YOU'RE ON THE RIGHT TRACK, THERE YOU GO AGAIN, WATCH YOUR STEP, I TOLD YOU SO. For each of them I could work out the calculation, the light-years from here to there, the light-years from there to here, and establish which episode they were referring to: all the actions of my life, every time I picked my nose, all the times I managed to jump down from a moving tram, were still there, traveling from one galaxy to another, and they were being considered, commented on, judged. The comments and judgments were not always pertinent: the sign TCHK TCHK applied to the time I gave a third of my salary to a charity subscription; the sign THIS TIME I LIKE YOU, to when I had forgotten in a train the manuscript of a treatise that had cost me years of study; my famous prolusion at the University of Göttingen was commented on with the words: WATCH OUT FOR DRAFTS.

In a certain sense, I could set my mind at rest: no action of mine, good or bad, was completely lost. At least an echo of it was always saved; or rather, several echoes, which varied from one end of the universe to the other, and in that sphere which was expanding and generating other spheres; but the echoes were discontinuous, conflicting pieces of information, inessential, from which the nexus of my actions didn't emerge, and a new action was unable to explain or correct an old one, so they remained one next to the other, with a plus or minus sign, like a long, long polynomial which cannot be reduced to a more simple expression.

What could I do, at this point? To keep bothering with the past was useless; so far it had gone the way it had gone; I had to make sure the future went better. The important thing was that, in everything I did, it should be clear what was essential, where the stress should be placed, what was to be noted and what not. I procured an enormous directional sign, one of those huge hands with the pointing index finger. When I performed an action to which I wanted to call attention, I had only to raise that sign, trying to make the finger point at the most important detail of the scene. For the moments when, instead, I preferred not to be observed, I made another sign, a hand with the thumb pointing in the direction opposite the one I was turning, to distract attention.

All I had to do was carry those signs wherever I went and raise one or the other, according to the occasion. It was a long-term operation, naturally: the observers hundreds of thousands of light-years away would be hundreds of thousands of millennia late in perceiving what I was doing now, and I would have to wait more hundreds of thousands of millennia to read their reactions. This delay was inevitable; but there was, unfortunately, another drawback I hadn't foreseen: what could I do when I realized I had raised the wrong sign?

For example, at a certain moment I was sure I was about to do something that would give me dignity and prestige; I hastened to wave the sign with the index finger pointed at me; and at that very moment I happened to make a dreadful faux pas, something unforgivable, a display of human wretchedness to make you sink into the ground in shame. But it was done; that image, with the pointing sign, was already navigating through space, nobody could stop it, it was devouring the light-years, spreading among the galaxies, arousing in the millions of future centuries comments and laughter and turned-up noses, which from the depths of the millennia would return to me and would force me to still clumsier excuses, to more embarrassed attempts at correction . . .

Another day, instead, I had to face an unpleasant situation, one of those situations in life that one is obliged to live through, knowing that, whatever happens, there's no way of showing up well. I shielded myself with the sign with the thumb pointing in the other way, and I went off. Unexpectedly, in that delicate and ticklish situation, I displayed quick-wittedness, a balance, a tact, a decisiveness that no one—myself least of all—had ever suspected in me: I suddenly revealed hidden talents that implied a long ripening of character; and meanwhile the sign was deflecting the observers' gaze, making them look at a pot of peonies nearby.

Cases like these, which at first I considered exceptions, the result of my inexperience, kept happening to me more and more frequently. Too late I realized I should have pointed out what I hadn't wanted seen and should have hidden what I had instead pointed out: there was no way to arrive before the image and to warn them not to pay attention to the sign.

I tried making a third sign with the word CORRECTION, to

raise when I wanted to annul the preceding sign, but in every galaxy this image would have been seen only after the one it was meant to correct, and by then the harm was done and I would only seem doubly ridiculous, and to neutralize that with another sign, IGNORE CORRECTION, would have been equally useless.

I went on living, waiting for the remote moment when, from the galaxies, the comments on the new episodes would arrive, charged for me with embarrassment and uneasiness; then I would be able to rebut, sending off my messages of reply, which I was already pondering, each dictated by the situation. Meanwhile, the galaxies for whom I was most compromised were already revolving around the threshold of the billions of light-years at such speeds that, to reach them, my messages would have to struggle across space, clinging to their accelerating flight: then, one by one, they would disappear from the last ten-billion-light-year horizon beyond which no visible object can be seen, and they would bear with them a judgment by then irrevocable.

And, thinking of this judgment I would no longer be able to change, I suddenly felt a kind of relief, as if peace could come to me only after the moment when there would be nothing to add and nothing to remove in that arbitrary ledger of misunderstandings, and the galaxies which were gradually reduced to the last tail of the last luminous ray, winding from the sphere of darkness, seemed to bring with them the only possible truth about myself, and I couldn't wait until all of them, one after the other, had followed this path.

THE SPIRAL

*F*or the majority of mollusks, the visible organic form has little importance in the life of the members of a species, since they cannot see one another and have, at most, only a vague perception of other individuals and of their surroundings. This does not prevent brightly colored stripings and forms which seem very beautiful to our eyes (as in many gastropod shells) from existing independently of any relationship to visibility.

I

Like me, when I was clinging to that rock, you mean?—*Qfwfq asked,*—With the waves rising and falling, and me there, still, flat, sucking what there was to suck and thinking about it all the time? If that's the time you want to know about, there isn't much I can tell you. Form? I didn't have any; that is, I didn't know I had one, or rather I didn't know you *could* have one. I grew more or less on all sides, at random; if this is what you call radial symmetry, I suppose I had radial symmetry, but to tell you the truth I never paid any attention to it. Why should I have grown more on one side than on the other? I had no eyes, no head, no part of the body that was different from any other part; now I try to persuade myself that the two holes I had were a mouth and an anus, and that I therefore already had my bilateral symmetry, just like the trilobites and the rest of you, but in my memory I really can't tell those holes apart, I passed stuff from whatever side I felt like, inside or outside was the same, differences and repugnances came along much later. Every now and then I was seized by fantasies, that's true; for example, the notion of scratching my armpit, or crossing my legs, or once even of growing a mustache. I use these words here with you, to make myself clear; then there were many details I couldn't foresee: I had some cells, one more or less the same as another, and they all did more or less the same job. But since I had no form I could feel all possible forms in myself, and all actions and expressions and possibilities of making noises, even rude ones. In short, there were no limitations to my thoughts, which weren't thoughts, after all, because I had no brain to think them; every cell on its own thought every thinkable thing all at once, not through images, since we had no images of any kind at our disposal, but simply in that indeterminate way of feeling oneself there, which did not prevent us from feeling ourselves equally there in some other way.

It was a rich and free and contented condition, my condition at that time, quite the contrary of what you might think. I was a bachelor (our system of reproduction in those days didn't require even temporary couplings), healthy, without too many ambitions. When you're young, all evolution lies before you, every road is open to you, and at the same time you can enjoy the fact of being there on the rock, flat mollusk-pulp, damp and happy. If you compare yourself with the limitations that came afterwards, if you think of how having one form excludes other forms, of the monotonous routine where you finally feel trapped, well, I don't mind saying life was beautiful in those days.

To be sure, I lived a bit withdrawn into myself, that's true, no comparison with our interrelated life nowadays; and I'll also admit that—partly because of my age and partly under the influence of my surroundings—I was what they call a narcissist to a slight extent; I mean I stayed there observing myself all the time, I saw all my good points and all my defects, and I liked myself for the former and for the latter; I had no terms of comparison, you must remember that, too.

But I wasn't so backward that I didn't know something else existed beyond me: the rock where I clung, obviously, and also the water that reached me with every wave, but other stuff, too, farther on: that is, the world. The water was a source of information, reliable and precise: it brought me edible substances which I absorbed through all my surface, and other inedible ones which still helped me form an idea of what there was

142

around. The system worked like this: a wave would come, and I, still sticking to the rock, would raise myself up a little bit, imperceptibly—all I had to do was loosen the pressure slightly —and, splat, the water passed beneath me, full of substances and sensations and stimuli. You never knew how those stimuli were going to turn out, sometimes a tickling that made you die laughing, other times a shudder, a burning, an itch; so it was a constant seesaw of amusement and emotion. But you mustn't think I just lay there passively, dumbly accepting everything that came: after a while I had acquired some experience and I was quick to analyze what sort of stuff was arriving and to decide how I should behave, to make the best use of it or to avoid the more unpleasant consequences. It was all a kind of game of contractions, with each of the cells I had, or of relaxing at the right moment: and I could make my choices, reject, attract, even spit.

And so I learned that there were *the others,* the element surrounding me was filled with traces of them, *others* hostile and different from me or else disgustingly similar. No, now I'm giving you a disagreeable idea of my character, which is all wrong. Naturally, each of us went about on his own business, but the presence of the *others* reassured me, created an inhabited zone around me, freed me from the fear of being an alarming exception, which I would have been if the fact of existing had been my fate alone, a kind of exile.

So I knew that some of the *others* were female. The water transmitted a special vibration, a kind of brrrum brrrum brrrum, I remember when I became aware of it the first time, or rather, not the first, I remember when I became aware of being aware of it as a thing I had always known. At the discovery of these vibrations' existence, I was seized with a great curiosity, not so much to see them, or to be seen by them either—since, first, we hadn't any sight, and secondly, the sexes weren't yet differentiated, each individual was identical with every other individual and at looking at one or another I would have felt no more pleasure than in looking at myself—but a curiosity to know whether something would happen between me and them. A desperation filled me, a desire not to do anything special, which would have been out of place, knowing that there was nothing special to do, or nonspecial either, but to respond in some way to that vibration with a corresponding vibration, or rather, with a personal vibration of my own, because, sure enough, there was something there that wasn't exactly the same as the other, I mean now you might say it came from hormones, but for me it was very beautiful.

So then, one of them, shlup shlup shlup, emitted her eggs, and I, shlup shlup shlup, fertilized them: all down inside the sea, mingling in the water tepid from the sun; oh, I forgot to tell you, I could feel the sun, which warmed the sea and heated the rock.

One of them, I said. Because, among all those female messages that the sea slammed against me like an indistinct soup at first where everything was all right with me and I grubbed about paying no attention to what one was like or another, suddenly I understood what corresponded best to my tastes, tastes which I hadn't known before that moment, of course. In other words, I had fallen in love. What I mean is: I had begun to recognize, to isolate the signs of one of those from the others, in fact I waited for these signs I had begun to recognize, I sought them, responded to those signs I awaited with other signs I made myself, or rather it was I who aroused them, these signs from her, which I answered with other signs of my own, I mean I was in love with her and she with me, so what more could I want from life?

Now habits have changed, and it already seems inconceivable to you that one could love a female like that, without having spent any time with her. And yet, through that unmistakable part of her still in solution in the sea water, which the waves placed at my disposal, I received a quantity of information about her, more than you can imagine: not the superficial, generic information you get now, seeing and smelling and touching and hearing a voice, but essential information, which I could then develop at length in my imagination. I could think of her with minute precision, thinking not so much of how she was made, which would have been a banal and vulgar way of

144

thinking of her, but of how from her present formlessness she would be transformed into one of the infinite possible forms, still remaining herself, however. I didn't imagine the forms that she might assume, but I imagined the special quality that, in taking them, she would give to those forms.

I knew her well, in other words. And I wasn't sure of her. Every now and then I was overcome with suspicion, anxiety, rage. I didn't let anything show, you know my character, but beneath that impassive mask passed suppositions I can't bring myself to confess even now. More than once I suspected she was unfaithful to me, that she sent messages not only to me but also to others; more than once I thought I had intercepted one, or that I had discovered a tone of insincerity in a message addressed to me. I was jealous, I can admit it now, not so much out of distrust of her as out of unsureness of myself: who could assure me that she had really understood who I was? Or that she had understood the fact that I was? This relationship achieved between us thanks to the sea water—a full, complete relationship, what more could I ask for?—was for me something absolutely personal, between two unique and distinct individualities; but for her? Who could assure me that what she might find in me she hadn't also found in another, or in another two or three or ten or a hundred like me? Who could assure me that her abandon in our shared relations wasn't an indiscriminate abandon, slapdash, a kind of—who's next?—collective ecstasy?

The fact that these suspicions did not correspond to the truth was confirmed, for me, by the subtle, soft, private vibration, at times still trembling with modesty, in our correspondences; but what if, precisely out of shyness and inexperience, she didn't pay enough attention to my characteristics and others took advantage of this innocence to worm their way in? And what if she, a novice, believed it was still I and couldn't distinguish one from the other, and so our most intimate play was extended to a circle of strangers . . .?

It was then that I began to secrete calcareous matter. I wanted to make something to mark my presence in an unmistakable fashion, something that would defend this individual presence of mine from the indiscriminate instability of all the rest. Now it's no use my piling up words, trying to explain the novelty of this intention I had; the first word I said is more than enough: *make,* I wanted to *make,* and considering the fact that I had never made anything or thought you could make anything, this in itself was a big event. So I began to make the first thing that occurred to me, and it was a shell. From the margin of that fleshy cloak on my body, using certain glands, I began to give off secretions which took on a curving shape all around, until I was covered with a hard and variegated shield, rough on the outside and smooth and shiny inside. Naturally, I had no way of controlling the form of what I was making: I just stayed there all huddled up, silent and sluggish, and I secreted. I went on even after the shell covered my whole body; I began another turn; in short, I was getting one of those shells all twisted into a spiral, which you, when you see them, think are so hard to make, but all you have to do is keep working and giving off the same matter without stopping, and they grow like that, one turn after the other.

Once it existed, this shell was also a necessary and indispensable place to stay inside of, a defense for my survival; it was a lucky thing I had made it, but while I was making it I had no idea of making it because I needed it; on the contrary, it was like when somebody lets out an exclamation he could perfectly well not make, and yet he makes it, like "Ha" or "hmph!," that's how I made the shell: simply to express myself. And in this self-expression I put all the thoughts I had about her, I released the anger she made me feel, my amorous way of thinking about her, my determination to exist for her, the desire for me to be me, and for her to be her, and the love for myself that I put in my love for her—all the things that could be said only in that conch shell wound into a spiral.

At regular intervals the calcareous matter I was secreting came out colored, so a number of lovely stripes were formed running straight through the spirals, and this shell was a thing different from me but also the truest part of me, the explanation of who I was, my portrait translated into a rhythmic system of volumes and stripes and colors and hard matter, and it was the portrait of her as she was, because at the same time she was making herself a shell identical to mine and without knowing it I was copying what she was doing and she without knowing it was copying what I was doing, and all the others were copying all the others, so we would be back where we had been before except for the fact that in saying these shells were the same I was a bit hasty, because when you looked closer you discovered all sorts of little differences that later on might become enormous.

So I can say that my shell made itself, without my taking any special pains to have it come out one way rather than another, but this doesn't mean that I was absent-minded during that time; I applied myself, instead, to that act of secreting, without allowing myself a moment's distraction, never thinking of anything else, or rather: thinking always of something else, since I didn't know how to think of the shell, just as, for that matter, I didn't know how to think of anything else either, but I accompanied the effort of making the shell with the effort of thinking I was making something, that is anything: that is, I thought of all the things it would be possible to make. So it wasn't even a monotonous task, because the effort of thinking which accompanied it spread toward countless types of thoughts which spread, each one, toward countless types of actions that might each serve to make countless things, and making each of these things was implicit in making the shell grow, turn after turn . . .

II

(And so now, after five hundred million years have gone by, I look around and, above the rock, I see the railway embankment and the train passing along it with a party of Dutch girls looking out of the window and, in the last compartment, a solitary traveler reading Herodotus in a bilingual edition, and the train vanishes into the tunnel under the highway, where there is a sign with the pyramids and the words "VISIT EGYPT," and a little ice-cream wagon tries to pass a big truck laden with

147

installments of Rh-Stijl, *a periodical encyclopedia that comes out in paperback, but then it puts its brakes on because its visibility is blocked by a cloud of bees which crosses the road coming from a row of hives in a field from which surely a queen bee is flying away, drawing behind her a swarm in the direction opposite to the smoke of the train, which has reappeared at the other end of the tunnel, so you can see hardly anything thanks to the cloudy stream of bees and coal smoke, except a few yards farther up there is a peasant breaking the ground with his mattock and, unaware, he brings to light and reburies a fragment of a Neolithic mattock similar to his own, in a garden that surrounds an astronomical observatory with its telescopes aimed at the sky and on whose threshold the keeper's daughter sits reading the horoscopes in a weekly whose cover displays the face of the star of* Cleopatra: *I see all this and I feel no amazement because making the shell implied also making the honey in the wax comb and the coal and the telescopes and the reign of Cleopatra and the films about Cleopatra and the pyramids and the design of the zodiac of the Chaldean astrologers and the wars and empires Herodotus speaks of and the words written by Herodotus and the works written in all languages including those of Spinoza in Dutch and the fourteen-line summary of Spinoza's life and works in the installment of the encyclopedia in the truck passed by the ice-cream wagon, and so I feel as if, in making the shell, I had also made the rest.*

I look around, and whom am I looking for? She is still the one I seek; I've been in love for five hundred million years, and if I see a Dutch girl on the sand with a beachboy wearing a gold chain around his neck and showing her the swarm of bees to frighten her, there she is: I recognize her from her inimitable way of raising one shoulder until it almost touches her cheek, I'm almost sure, or rather I'd say absolutely sure if it weren't for a certain resemblance that I find also in the daughter of the keeper of the observatory, and in the photograph of the actress made up as Cleopatra, or perhaps in Cleopatra as she really was in person, for what part of the true Cleopatra they say every representation of Cleopatra contains, or in the queen bee flying at the head of the swarm with that forward impetu-

ousness, or in the paper woman cut out and pasted on the plastic windshield of the little ice-cream wagon, wearing a bathing suit like the Dutch girl on the beach now listening over a little transistor radio to the voice of a woman singing, the same voice that the encyclopedia truck driver hears over his radio, and the same one I'm now sure I've heard for five million years, it is surely she I hear singing and whose image I look for all around, seeing only gulls volplaning on the surface of the sea where a school of anchovies glistens and for a moment I am certain I recognize her in a female gull and a moment later I suspect that instead she's an anchovy, though she might just as well be any queen or slave-girl named by Herodotus or only hinted at in the pages of the volume left to mark the seat of the reader who has stepped into the corridor of the train to strike up a conversation with the party of Dutch tourists; I might say I am in love with each of those girls and at the same time I am sure of being in love always with her alone.

And the more I torment myself with love for each of them, the less I can bring myself to say to them: "Here I am!," afraid of being mistaken and even more afraid that she is mistaken, taking me for somebody else, for somebody who, for all she knows of me, might easily take my place, for example the beach-boy with the gold chain, or the director of the observatory, or a gull, or a male anchovy, or the reader of Herodotus, or Herodotus himself, or the vendor of ice cream, who has come down to the beach along a dusty road among the prickly pears and is now surrounded by the Dutch girls in their bathing suits, or Spinoza, or the truck driver who is transporting the life and works of Spinoza summarized and repeated two thousand times, or one of the drones dying at the bottom of the hive after having fulfilled his role in the continuation of the species.)

III

. . . Which doesn't mean that the shell wasn't, first and foremost, a shell, with its particular form, which couldn't be any different because it was the very form I had given it, the only one I could or would give it. Since the shell had a form, the form of the world was also changed, in the sense that now it included the form of the world as it had been without a shell plus the form of the shell.

And that had great consequences: because the waving vibrations of light, striking bodies, produce particular effects from them, color first of all, namely, that matter I used to make stripes with which vibrated in a different way from the rest; but there was also the fact that a volume enters into a special relationship of volumes with other volumes, all phenomena I couldn't be aware of, though they existed.

The shell in this way was able to create visual images of shells, which are things very similar—as far as we know—to the shell itself, except that the shell is here, whereas the images of it are formed elsewhere, possibly on a retina. An image therefore presupposes a retina, which in turn presupposes a complex system stemming from an encephalon. So, in producing the shell, I also produced its image—not one, of course, but many, because with one shell you can make as many shell-images as you want—but only potential images because to form an image you need all the requisites I mentioned before: an encephalon with its optic ganglia, and an optic nerve to carry the vibrations from outside to inside, and this optic nerve, at the other extremity, ends in something made purposely to see what there is outside, namely the eye. Now it's ridiculous to think that, having an encephalon, one would simply drop a nerve like a fishing line cast into the darkness; until the eyes crop up, one can't know whether there is something to be seen outside or not. For myself, I had none of this equipment, so I was the least authorized to speak of it; however, I had conceived an idea of my own, namely that the important thing was to form some visual images, and the eyes would come later in consequence. So I concentrated on making the part of me that was outside (and even the interior part of me that conditioned the exterior) give rise to an image, or rather to what would later be called a lovely image (when compared to other images considered less lovely, or rather ugly, or simply revoltingly hideous).

When a body succeeds in emitting or in reflecting luminous vibrations in a distinct and recognizable order—I thought—what does it do with these vibrations? Put them in its pocket? No, it releases them on the first passer-by. And how will the latter behave in the face of vibrations he can't utilize and which, taken in this way, might even be annoying? Hide his head in a hole? No, he'll thrust it out in that direction until the point most exposed to the optic vibrations becomes sensitized and develops the mechanism for exploiting them in the form of images. In short, I conceived of the eye-encephalon link as a kind of tunnel dug from the outside by the force of what was ready to become image, rather than from within by the intention of picking up any old image.

And I wasn't mistaken: even today I'm sure that the project —in its over-all aspect—was right. But my error lay in thinking that sight would also come to us, that is to me and to her. I elaborated a harmonious, colored image of myself to enter her visual receptivity, to occupy its center, to settle there, so that she could utilize me constantly, in dreaming and in memory, with thought as well as with sight. And I felt at the same time she was radiating an image of herself so perfect that it would impose itself on my foggy, backward senses, developing in me an interior visual field where it would blaze forth definitely.

So our efforts led us to become those perfect objects of a sense whose nature nobody quite knew yet, and which later became perfect precisely through the perfection of its object, which was, in fact, us. I'm talking about sight, the eyes; only I had failed to foresee one thing: the eyes that finally opened to see us didn't belong to us but to others.

Shapeless, colorless beings, sacks of guts stuck together care-lessly, peopled the world all around us, without giving the slightest thought to what they should make of themselves, to how to express themselves and identify themselves in a stable, complete form, such as to enrich the visual possibilities of who-ever saw them. They came and went, sank a while, then emerged, in that space between air and water and rock, wan-dering about absently; and we in the meanwhile, she and I and all those intent on squeezing out a form of ourselves, were there slaving away at our dark task. Thanks to us, that badly defined space became a visual field; and who reaped the benefit? These intruders, who had never before given a thought to the possibility of eyesight (ugly as they were, they wouldn't have gained a thing by seeing one another), these creatures who had always turned a deaf ear to the vocation of form. While we were bent over, doing the hardest part of the job, that is, creating something to be seen, they were quietly taking on the easiest part: adapting their lazy, embryonic receptive organs to what there was to receive; our images. And they needn't try telling me now that their job was toilsome too: from that gluey mess that filled their heads anything could have come out, and a photosensitive mechanism doesn't take all that much trouble to put together. But when it comes to perfecting it, that's another story! How can you, if you don't have visible objects to see, gaudy ones even, the kind that impose themselves on the eyesight? To sum it up in a few words: they developed eyes at our expense.

So sight, *our* sight, which we were obscurely waiting for, was the sight that the others had of us. In one way or another, the great revolution had taken place: all of a sudden, around us, eyes were opening, and corneas and irises and pupils: the swollen, colorless eye of polyps and cuttlefish, the dazed and gelatinous eyes of bream and mullet, the protruding and peduncled eyes of crayfish and lobsters, the bulging and faceted eyes of flies and ants. A seal now comes forward, black and shiny, winking little eyes like pinheads. A snail extends ball-like eyes at the end of long antennae. The inexpressive eyes of the gull examine the surface of the water. Beyond a glass mask the frowning eyes of an underwater fisherman explore the depths. Through the lens of a spyglass a sea captain's eyes and the eyes of a woman bathing converge on my shell, then look at each other, forgetting me. Framed by far-sighted lenses I feel on me the far-sighted eyes of a zoologist, trying to frame me in the eye of a Rolleiflex. At that moment a school of tiny anchovies, barely born, passes before me, so tiny that in each little white fish it seems there is room only for the eye's black dot, and it is a kind of eye-dust that crosses the sea.

All these eyes were mine. I had made them possible; I had had the active part; I furnished them the raw material, the image. With eyes had come all the rest, so everything that the others, having eyes, had become, their every form and function, and the quantity of things that, thanks to eyes, they had managed to do, in their every form and function, came from what I had done. Of course, they were not just casually implicit in my being there, in my having relations with others, male and female, et cetera, in my setting out to make a shell, et cetera. In other words, I had foreseen absolutely everything.

And at the bottom of each of those eyes I lived, or rather another me lived, one of the images of me, and it encountered the image of her, the most faithful image of her, in that beyond which opens, past the semiliquid sphere of the irises, in the darkness of the pupils, the mirrored hall of the retinas, in our true element which extends without shores, without boundaries.